The Change¹⁰

Insights into Self-Empowerment

Jim Britt ~ Jim Lutes

With

Co-authors From Around the World

The Change^{10}

Jim Britt ~ Jim Lutes

All Rights Reserved

Copyright 2016

The Change

10556 Combie Road, Suite 6205

Auburn, CA 95602

The use of any part of this publication, whether reproduced, stored in any retrieval system or transmitted in any forms or by any means, electronic or otherwise, without the prior written consent of the publisher, is an infringement of copyright law.

Jim Lutes ~ Jim Britt

The Change^{10}

ISBN:

Print: 978-1-4951-9789-5
Ebook: 978-1-4951-9790-1

Co-authors

Julia A. Nicholson

Kim Malama Lucien

David Musgrave

Cliff Waterbury

David Heavener

Jo Condrill

Nomi Bachar

Mindy Anderson

Stuart Elliott

Mache Torres

Terry Nadine Taylor

Josephine Harewood

Beth Haley

Neil Millard

Katie Macks

Jenny Beilsmith

Michelle Gesky

Sally Kay Miller

Pamela & W.T. Hamilton

Calvin Carey

The Change is proud to support Good Women International

Every five minutes, one American child (many as young as ten years old) will be abducted and trafficked into the sex trade. 274 children a day. 100,000 each year and that estimate could be low. The total current number of human trafficking victims in the U.S. alone reaches into the hundreds of thousands and worldwide into the millions.

All profits from the sale of Amazon Kindle electronic books are being donated to Good Women International, whose focus is on the prevention of sexual exploitation of young women and children. They support self-empowerment and educational programs worldwide designed to educate our youth to avoid becoming a victim. A recent successful project was an anti-trafficking curricula for our high schools which is now complete.

Enslavement is a reality. It is documented and it is real. The question is: What are we going to do about it?

To make a donation to Good Women International, a non-profit subsidiary of Village Care International, go to: www.SupportGoodWomen.com. All donations are tax deductible under Tax ID #: 88-0471768. We welcome and appreciate your donations no matter how small.

http://GoodWomenInternational.org

Note: *Donations are never for salaries, as Good Women is a volunteer organization.*

DEDICATION

This book is dedicated to all those seeking change

Foreword

Berny Dohrmann,

Chairman of CEO Space International

To The Readers of *The Change* Series:

Jim Britt has been a mentor to *Chicken Soup* authors, and to some of the foremost thought leaders on earth. Jim Britt's groundbreaking work in *Letting Go*, releasing past traumas and betrayals in life to return once again to forward-looking manifestation within your full powers, has been instructing at leading *Fortune* companies and to standing-room-only seminars all over the world. For three decades, Jim Britt has been the "trainer of the trainers," of which I am only one. Jim has been an instructor at CEO Space, the most prestigious, hard to get into faculty on the planet, where he developed millions of dollars of resources as he assisted others to develop tens of millions of dollars for their own dream making. Jim is the most "unchanged by success and wealth" man I have ever known. He is an unselfish archangel, like in his book *Rings of Truth*.

Today, Jim Britt and Jim Lutes, along with many inspiring co-authors from around the world, bring a pioneering work to the market to transform your own journey into master manifestation. Their principles are forged on coaching millions on every continent. As you read, you are exploring self-development as the world has yet to practice. In fact, Jim and Jim's publications lead to this one APEX MOMENT. Everything you have done to date in your own life, everyone you have met, every lesson you have learned, has led you to this one GREAT life opportunity… the moment of your own transformation into ever-rising full potentials.

As a five-time best-selling author myself, as a filmmaker, and with CEO Space, you can imagine how fussy I am to write a foreword to publications in the self-development space. CEO Space was just ranked by *Forbes Magazine* as the leading entrepreneur firm, which hosts five annual business growth conferences serving over 140 countries. It was also named by *Forbes* as THE MEETING in the world that YOU CANNOT AFFORD TO MISS. The world today demands more than a reputation defender to secure your forward brand; it requires that you take responsibility for your own brand and reputation in life. This book will inspire you to do just that.

CEO Space International has supported launches for many amazing works, including Chicken Soup for the Soul; Men Are From Mars, Women Are From Venus; Rich Dad, Poor Dad; The Secret; No Matter What; Three Feet From Gold; Conversations With The King; and now the movies Growing Up Graceland and Wish Man (for Make a Wish Foundation); Outwitting the Devil by Napoleon Hill and Sharon Lechter; Tony Robbins' great publications; of course Jim Britt's best-selling book Rings of Truth; and so many more. The totals have reached more than 2 billion eyeballs! You can't play around with that Mount Everest of credibility that I guard like a bank vault!

You can therefore appreciate why I encourage 100% of our followers of all the publications named to BUY JIM BRITT and JIM LUTES' book series *The Change* as a customer recognition for your own ten-best close relationships or clients. But don't just buy this book; rather, I endorse that you buy 10, and you giftwrap them to acknowledge your most important top ten relationships in life or clients in business. By doing so, you will retain more clients and encourage repeat buying. You may also receive more referrals and strengthen each relationship. The laws of giving will come back to you 10 to 1. When you give freely, you will always receive a rain into your life just as you rain into the lives of those you treasure. Jim Britt, Jim Lutes, and the insightful and inspiring co-authors have given you in *The Change* series a great opportunity… more important than pouring ice water over someone's head on YouTube as a challenge for charity! The gift that keeps on giving begins when you step up and BUY 10, knowing you have been instrumental in inspiring 10 friends to live a better life. Together, we are going to reach 1 BILLION SOULS as we help Jim Britt, Jim Lutes, and their co-authors to achieve their goal to transform human consciousness in our lifetime. Like Zig Ziglar, Jim Rohn, the great Roger Anthony, and so many friends who have passed, my friend Jim Britt is now a historical event in every training, every publication, and every online work at CEO Space. If you ever have the opportunity, STOP YOUR LIFE and see JIM BRITT & JIM LUTES LIVE and you will thank me personally, I know.

Their work is powerful. You'll let go of the baggage you've been carrying around for years and learn to embrace everything that creates the future you want and deserve. As you close the pages of any of *The Change* books, you will say over and over again "THANK YOU Jim Britt and Jim Lutes for creating this work." You will gain a new life of super focus as never before and you will commence to master manifest in your own individual life as never before. *The Change* books provide tools to transform results for corporations, institutions, and individuals, and once applied it will be impossible to miss your future success in life.

In my opinion, there are only the following areas to embrace for each of us:

Spiritual oneness and balance

Recreational balance and nature

Relationship where *Perfection Can Be Had!* (my book)

Career attainment of goals that you, yourself, reset along the way

Parenting either directly or by embracing a child you adopt to mentor at any and every age in life

These perspectives come into alignment within a framework of Jim Britt and Jim Lutes' imagination, along with decades of human-potential work. My advice is this work is a "BUY 10 TO SHARE WITH FRIENDS" pledge. In fact, a billion readers is a global path that Jim Britt and Jim Lutes are going to achieve NEXT for the world common good.

Let's help in this quest, as both men unselfishly donate their only asset, their precious LIFE TIME, to elevate one life at a time to their full potential and greatness.

My final request to all those who are reading my foreword is that you DO IT NOW. When you think of the good you will be doing, just ask yourself, "How long will I make them WAIT?"

I'm buying my 10 today!

Berny Dohrmann

Chairman, CEO Space International

P.S. I so approve this message for all my readers and followers worldwide. CEO Space has helped authors break the book of all records a half a dozen times, which means the only record to beat can be done with the publication you are buying 10 of now. Together, we are going to set a global record with one publication. Make the PLEDGE and give the gift of personal development. DO IT TODAY!

Table of Contents

Foreword vii

Jim Britt.. 1
    What ALL Wealthy People Have in Common

Jim Lutes 23
    It's Not Where You Are, It's Where You're Going

Julia A. Nicholson 31
    The Moment Everything Changes

Beth Haley 43
    Change through Choice: Choosing to Create the Relationship You Want

David Heavener 55
    Your Life is a Movie: Lights. Camera. *Take* Action.

Cliff Waterbury 65
    Walking Between Two Worlds

Jennifer Beilsmith 77
    The Power Within

Josephine Harewood 87
    Wake up! Wake up!

Kim Malama Lucien 99
> Benevolent Leadership: Creating Growth & Sustainability through Empowerment

Jo Condrill 109
> How To Reinvent Yourself In 7 Simple Steps

Mache Torres 121
> Explore The Deepest Essence of Your Being

Mindy Anderson 133
> Lead Yourself First Before You Lead Others

Pamela Hamilton and W.T. Hamilton 145
> Warning, Take a Deep Breath: You're About to Learn How to Make the Impossible Possible

Neil Millard 157
> What BC Did For Me

Nomi Bachar 167
> You Are The Source: Are You Walking in Your Big Shoes?

David Musgrave 179
> TAKE CHARGE of your Happiness, Belly fat, and Sexiness: A Woman's Route to Wellness

Sally Kay Miller 193
> My Journey to Getting my HOPE back, After Losing my Child to Addiction

Terry Nadine Taylor 203

    Liberate the Leader in You

Michelle Gesky 217

    The "Sh#*%" Word

Stuart Elliott 229

    Building Core Confidence

Katie Macks 241

    A Glowing Road Trip

Calvin Carey 251

    Where Are You? Looking at the world around you

Afterword 259

Jim Britt

Jim Britt is an internationally recognized leader in the field of peak performance and personal empowerment training. He is author of 13 best-selling books, including *Cracking the Rich Code; Cracking the Life Code; Rings of Truth; The Power of Letting Go; Freedom; Unleashing Your Authentic Power; Do This. Get Rich-For Entrepreneurs; The Flaw in The Law of Attraction;* and *The Law of Realization,* to name a few.

Jim has presented seminars throughout the world sharing his success principles and life-enhancing realizations with thousands of audiences, totaling over 1,000,000 people from all walks of life.

Jim has served as a success counselor to over 300 corporations worldwide. He was recently named as one of the world's top 20 success coaches and presented with the best of the best award out of the top 100 contributors of all time to the direct selling industry. He also mentored/coached Anthony Robbins for his first five years in business.

Jim is more than aware of the challenges we all face in making adaptive changes for a sustainable future.

What ALL Wealthy People Have in Common

By Jim Britt

What's the secret to incredible financial success? The secret is, there is no <u>one</u> secret! The reality is there are many "secrets" that work together in combination with one another—giving you the winning "combination" to succeed! Think of success like a giant vault at the bank with a thick steel door blocking it and a combination lock. Unless you have the right combination to that lock, it doesn't matter how much you beat on the door, how hard you work, how many lists you make or good intentions you have, because there is a combination you must know to unlock that door and get it to swing open so you can walk through to the other side. In this chapter, I'll be sharing a couple of those success secrets with you… some straight-talk keys that make the difference between struggling your whole life in frustration, or becoming wealthy.

Many years ago, I met a very wealthy person and I asked what inspired him to be wealthy. His answer really surprised me. "Money is a game and the man with the most notches on his belt wins." I was shocked! I was a young man at the time and having grown up without much, I wanted to become rich. Yet after hearing this person's response, I looked deeper into his eyes and frankly, he didn't seem all that happy and the sense of lack of balance in his life was apparent. He was out of shape and had a look in his eyes of anxiety, loneliness, and anger. I could tell that he had stepped on a lot of people to get to where he was.

How about you? Do you think that being financially wealthy takes putting yourself first and tramping over those that get in your way? Do you think that being wealthy means putting the lust for money ahead of everything else?

I've also met very wealthy people who give back to their community, have large circles of friends, and always seemed to be abundant in so many other ways.

In fact, a year or so ago, I took a camera crew around the country and interviewed 11 self-made mega millionaires and one billionaire. The requirement was that they all had to have started with nothing. In other words, they didn't inherit their wealth. And all 12 made their money in different industries…internet marketing, traditional business, real estate, television, direct sales, social media, etc. If you asked any of these twelve individuals the same question, you'd likely get this sort of answer: "Wealth is simply a vehicle that magnifies your deeper personality traits and mindset."

If you are a good person, access to resources, such as these type of people, will only make you a better one. If your nature is negative, it will also magnify your unhealthy attributes on the downside and you will find yourself hanging around others that will support you in your negativity.

The following is what I have learned from my own experiences and the experiences of these 12 mega-millionaires, as well as others I have associated myself with over the past 40 years.

Wealth is the ultimate power of leverage. Nothing is truer about becoming and deciding to become wealthy. It is a magnifying glass into your soul.

I have tried to model myself after this philosophy, never forgetting that money is simply a means to achieving larger and greater things in life. After all, if the only reason you are pursuing buckets of money is to swim in it like Scrooge McDuck, you may find yourself the richest person in a very unhappy world.

Wouldn't it be nice if you could simply decide to become wealthy and you did?

Well, let me fill you in on a big secret...YOU CAN!

You already know the basics. You know that you should pay off your debt and start budgeting. You know that all you need to do is regularly invest money into your savings and let time do the work. Spend less, save more, build your investment portfolio...you've heard it time and time again. Then why aren't you on the way to becoming wealthy?

There are many reasons that people don't take action, even though they have the information. The reality is that so many people are just simply afraid to change. Fear takes a lot away from a person. They don't want to fail but when you buy into fear, it will take you down that path.

Here's one key. For things to change for you financially, you have to make a change; otherwise you'll continue to keep producing the same results you've been producing. This may come as a shock to you, but most people really don't want to change. Just give them a beer, point them toward the sofa, and give them the television remote. They will continue to complacently live out their lives.

Most people are much too busy earning a living to become financially free. They spend the majority of their time focused on what they *don't have,* what they *don't want,* and on how to pay the bills, instead of focusing on what they *do have* and what they *do want* in their lives.

I know people, as I'm sure you do, that love having the drama of being up to their ears in debt. It's a balance beam that keeps excitement in their lives. It's a roller coaster ride that is thrilling, but always drops them off at the same place time and time again. But at such a huge cost! What they don't realize is that they can't maintain their balance or thrill forever. At some point, you have to decide where to get off.

I've often wondered, as I'm sure you have, why two people with the very same background and experience in the same type of business…one gains wealth, while the other barely survives? What determines the difference between someone who earns $50,000 and someone who earns $500,000 a year? Is it their education, their experience, the amount of money they have already, or is it simply a lucky break?

One of the things I discovered in my 40-year career is that successful people do things in a different way. To put it yet another way…they do things that the majority of people are not willing to do. Most have been conditioned to believe that creating wealth is difficult, or that it's only for the lucky few. What do you believe?

Everyone wants greater financial success, but the statistics say that most will never have it. Get this…this is shocking! According to the U.S. Social Security Administration, the average retired couple has less than $7,000 in savings. At retirement, 45% will depend on extra money from relatives for their survival. 30% depend on charity. 20% will still be working, and only 5% will be self-sustaining.

Wow! I don't know about you, but I find this unbelievable and even frightening!

I'm sure that people never believe, or even think, this would ever happen to them, but statistics say it will! So, according to statistics, at age 65, you'll still be working for someone else and with no nest egg to retire or depending on relatives to survive. I don't think people plan for this to happen. No one in their right mind would make a plan like that. They simply don't have a plan for it *not* to happen. They convince themselves that "someday" they are going to be a success, to start their own business, to make a financial plan for their future, to have all they want in life…someday.

Someday…what an interesting concept. Think of all the things that were supposed to have happened by now…that someday that you may have convinced yourself was just around the corner. To most, that someday is where we've convinced ourselves we would be right now, if only we had more time, more talent, more education, more money, or maybe a better opportunity available.

How about you…is your level of financial success today where you thought it would be five years ago? Before going any further, I would urge you to stop right now and take a realistic look at your last five years. Have you truly made progress? Are the last five years what *you* wanted? Are you where you thought you'd be today? And, most importantly, do you have a solid plan for the next five?

You and I both know that there are no guarantees in life, but I'm going to suggest to you is what you've probably already concluded…for things to change in your life, you have to make a change. I want to help you to make the changes necessary to have all you want in life.

Too many people like to complain, but just don't want to make the effort. They don't have time. They'll do it next year. Let me tell you, you have to find time to get your financial situation in order if you want to gain wealth. Time is costing you money. The more time you spend trying to pay off credit cards, the more you pay the credit card company and contribute to their wealth.

I'm not saying to ignore your financial obligations. What I'm saying is that paying off your credit cards, although a good place to start, will not bring you wealth. Why? Because after you pay them off, you are still left with the mentality that charged them to the max in the first place.

Don't let denial, fear, laziness, procrastination, or a need for drama get in your way of your wealth plan. You *can* have all the money you want. It just takes learning and developing the traits that rich people use, and some time to make it happen. The pathway to wealth is something you can absolutely choose to take.

To become wealthy, you will need some vital traits. Let me offer you a few.

First is a firm decision to become wealthy. Wealthy people you'll find make solid decisions and commit to seeing them through. Those who are not financially successful put off decisions or mess around with their decision once it is made.

The first step in becoming financially successful is making the decision to become wealthy…one that doesn't allow for anything less. Mediocrity is not an option to the wealthy. A decision creates a mindset, and a mindset makes you as mechanical and predictable as a calculator. Hit this number and it appears on the screen. Better yet, decide on a number and it appears in your bank account. It's really surprising though how many people don't like to make decisions. They do all sorts of things to keep the moment of decision at arm's length including: Gathering more data. Getting ready to get going…as soon as…Talking to more people. Getting other's opinions. Not thinking about the decision. Fretting over who the decision might offend. Worrying about the resources needed to pull off the decision. Or hoping they'll just get lucky and make the money they need without making a decision, etc.

The real problem is that most are stuck in a comfort zone and making a decision would possibly mean having to do something different that might be a bit painful. That's a decision we all face…the pain of staying stuck in our current situation or the pain of change. Most people would rather live with the "old you" for fear that becoming the "new you" would be too painful.

The Change[10]

Let's say a person makes a decision to be wealthy. What happens next when the old programs, the old habit patterns, and mind chatter kicks in? "Wait a minute! What makes you think you have the talent to become wealthy?" "I've never done it before! Maybe I really can't become wealthy." "I don't have the expertise, time, money, etc. to become wealthy." And before long, all the "self-talk" has pulled you off course and changed your decision into something totally different from becoming wealthy. Sound familiar? We all do it to some degree.

Remember this: <u>every income level requires a different you</u>. You have to be willing to let go of the "old you" and embrace the challenge of becoming the "new you." And, if you want to learn, grow, and change, you have to hang around people that challenge you to become better. If you want to become a million-dollar-a-year earner, but yet you hang around and take input from people earning $60,000 a year, you'll likely to be right where they are financially. If you want to become a million-dollar-a-year earner, *you have to make a decision to change*, and then you have to hang around million-dollar-a-year earners. Otherwise, there will always be somebody offering you the wrong input and telling you how to run your life, making you feel insecure and doubtful.

I know people, as I'm sure you do, who go to work every day to a job that they hate. They hate what they earn and/or what they do, but they stay because they feel they have no other choice. They justify their position by calling it job security. But what they don't realize is that there is no security in a job! It's called *prolonged poverty* in my book!

It's like living in a place you hate, but you're afraid to move because of your job. Then you lose your job and can't afford to move, so you look for another insecure position that will keep you in the place you hate. *That's a sort of insanity, don't you think?*

What would I say to a person in that position? *"If you want to get better, you have to make better decisions, and you have to hang out with and take input from those who've done it."* I would say, "If you want to be rich, you have to stop working for someone else's goals and dreams and make a decision to start working for your own. You have to stop with the employee mentality and start thinking like wealthy people think."

So, the next time you catch yourself saying, "I have no choice," stop and ask yourself if that's really true. The more you make choices that move you in the direction of your objective, the faster you will arrive there. The faster you get input from someone that's in the position you want to be, the faster you'll get there.

Here's the key—it is your job to make the decision, one that doesn't allow for anything less. It's not your job to figure out how you will attain wealth until the decision is made. Your initial job is to make a firm decision. Up until the decision is made, nothing happens…except, of course, the decision to stay where you are now. In reality, not making a decision is a decision to leave everything status quo.

Let me ask you a question. Let's say that there are two components that make up 100% of your financial success. Those two components are "decision" and "opportunity, or financial vehicle." My question is this: what percentage do each play in your financial success? When I ask a group this question, some say 50/50. Some say 80/20 and others say 20/80. What do you think? Here's the answer. It's 100% decision and 0% vehicle. Because without a firm decision, the vehicle doesn't matter in the least. Because without the decision, there will be no success, no matter what the vehicle. In fact, without the decision to become wealthy, there is no reason to even search for the vehicle. That would be like shopping for something that you have no interest in having.

Rich people develop the skill of making the best decision possible with the best information possible in the timeliest manner possible. They are quick to decide and quick to take responsibility for their decisions—positive or negative.

The next trait all wealthy people have in common is that they are bold. Financially successful people have learned that action is vital. And often times that requires a level of boldness. They know that procrastination kills. They live with the reality of consequences and know there will always be uncertainty in decisions, but they boldly step forward and make the decision anyway.

No one can see all possible ramifications; no one can predict every contingency; no one can absolutely prevent failure. The wealth-minded person knows that failure is not final; it's just one of those possible outcomes that happens on their way to success.

The real danger surrounding decision-making is not "will I make the wrong decision" but "did I make the best decision possible given the facts and circumstances." Success-minded individuals invest in learning what they need to make the correct decisions from those who have done what they want to do.

But, when it comes to investing in mentorship, so often I hear people say "I can't afford it." "It costs too much." When in reality, they can't afford not to. Wealthy people look at value, not cost. What will the investment make them rather than what it will cost them?

The success-minded, bold person will always recover from poor decisions—they know that they'll learn and become wiser, while the meek minded will mess around and miss opportunities, saying "I don't have the time. I don't have the money. The timing is not right, etc." And when they finally do make a decision, chances are their decision will have no momentum, no passion, and no urgency. If you wait for everything to be right before you decide, chances are you'll miss the opportunity altogether.

The real question is, "what do you really want?" Are you like most everyone who is obsessed with success, with having more money, more things, and better futures for themselves and their family?

Are you intrigued by the top companies: success stories of rags to riches, who's the coolest, the hottest, the richest, the boldest? Are you just dreaming about success or standing on the sidelines observing other people's successes and wishing you had what they have? Do you justify why you aren't financially successful? Or are you bold enough to step out in the spotlight and take center stage before you have all the answers?

The real questions are: "Do you want to be rich?" "Do you want to retire wealthy?" "What would financial success look like to you?" Most people have never defined what financial success would be for them, and they've never made a decision to have it. And that's the only reason they don't have it! The most important question that you can ask yourself is, "have I defined what financial success means to me…or am I just working for someone else's success and letting them define my level of financial worth?" Or are you basing your future financial success on past experiences? How you answer that question can change your life!

Often times, there is a feature in the investment section of some Sunday local newspapers. It's a success story column on people who've made it big financially in a respective business. You can also find those stories in magazines like *Entrepreneur* or *Inc*. You'll find stories of individuals who have carved out a niche for themselves in selected fields, lived a fulfilled life serving others with their skills, and amassed quite a fortune while doing so. You'll always find one common trait in all the featured personalities. Not one of them. Not some of them. But this trait is in all of them! It's called a "wealth mindset." Despite the fact that they're from different backgrounds, all of them possess the same mindset when it comes to money. Wealthy people think differently. This is the infamous "money consciousness" that most of the motivational and personal development trainers speak of so often in their books and seminars.

This wealthy mindset basically means this:

Regardless of the physical condition that you may be currently in, as long as you see yourself bathing in financial abundance, your actions will maneuver and circumstances will unfold in a way to create the wealth that you see yourself enjoying. If you possess the wealthy mindset, you will have the "Midas" touch when it comes to earning money. If you don't, you won't. It's that simple. The fortunate thing is, all of us possess the innate ability to fire up this wealthy mindset. But the key is letting go of the old you and holding true to the new you that you want to become. First is making the decision to be wealthy. Second is being bold. Next is letting go of your limiting beliefs about money.

Some people frown at the mere mention of money. How many times have you heard people say something like this: "oh, I'm not doing this for the money" or "Money isn't everything." Well, they're not wrong. Money isn't everything. The fact is that money in itself has no value. It's the things that money can buy when in circulation that makes it so valuable. Money can buy material possessions and personal freedom, and we all deserve to have what we want.

At the same time, if you look from a different angle, once you've got enough money to be financially free, it can literally change what you do from laborious work to spending more precious moments with your family and friends as well as doing the things you love.

Money can also allow you to contribute to a charity and benefit the less privileged.

On the other end of the scale, some people tend to overvalue the importance of money so much so that they become slaves to it. They love money so much that they let this passion cause their downfall…we've all witnessed it.

In essence, if you never come to terms with what money can bring forth into your life, its real value, and your uneasiness with the "idea" of money, it will limit your ability to attract more of it. To put it simply, just imagine this: Would you go into a car showroom if you've never had the intention to purchase a car? You may not want to buy it now, but the fact that you walked into the showroom implies that you appreciate the value of what a car brings. It can serve as a means of transportation for you and your family. And because of the perceived value you see to owning a car, you'll find the means and ways to get one. Having money is the same. Once you see its value and believe you can have it, you'll find the ways and means to getting it.

Remember, you can't create something that you're not in harmony with or that you haven't decided to have. Therefore, it becomes imperative that before you move on to other steps to really get this wealthy mindset concept. You should definitely have a conversation with yourself, or someone that can mentor you, to let go of the beliefs that are limiting you about money.

Having money means…finish the sentence…

What came up? Do you feel your answer will move you toward being wealthy?

Answer these questions:

Why do you deserve to be wealthy?

What do you believe about money?

How did you come to believe this?

Who taught you to believe that way?

Were they wealthy?

Who taught them?

The only way to change a belief is to challenge it. A belief is something that you have decided is true…it may not be at all. A belief is simply a decision that something is true. The good news is that you can change a belief simply by changing your decisions and letting go of the old you.

If you want to be wealthy, you have to first decide to be wealthy—whatever being wealthy means to you. Next is to decide "why" you want to be wealthy. What's the payoff for wealth? Your "why" is the fuel that will take you where you want to go. It's the passion behind the decision.

Everyone has the right to be wealthy. YOU have the right to be wealthy….and yet, most allow a temporary lack of money to eat into our minds, literally confining them into the vicious cycle of mediocrity.

The bottom line is that people are poor because they have not yet decided to be wealthy. To put it another way…mediocre earners are mediocre earners because they have decided to be.

So long as you make a conscious decision to become wealthy, have utmost faith that you can achieve it, and you let go of your outdated beliefs about money, you will act accordingly to what you believe. Why not say "yes" to getting wealthy today! And say it with conviction.

Deciding to be wealthy only gets you started on the quest. But what sustains you throughout the journey is the "why" you want to be wealthy and letting go of the mind chatter that pulls you back into your old habit patterns.

What is the reason that you want an extra $1 million in your bank account or you want to earn a million dollars a year? Why do you want to work your butt off, sacrificing your weekends to work a business or a job that only allows you to get by financially, when there is so much more available to you?

If you do not have a burning desire supporting your decision, and you don't let go of your old way of thinking and believing, you'll find your inspiration tapering off sooner and your decision fading into something totally different to being wealthy.

That's the trap that most everyone falls into.

Try this exercise. Take a piece of paper and scribble down all the reasons that you can think of why you want to be wealthy. Maybe you'd like to retire earlier and travel around the world? Or you want to quit your job and be a full-time parent? Write down as many why's as you can think of. Needless to say, the one that resonates with the deepest part of your heart should be written on an index card to remind you of the outcome you desire.

You'll also want to determine what wealth is to you. How much you want will inadvertently determine the action that you'll need to set forth to reach it.

Wealth can be whatever you say it is. For some, it might mean $10 million in the bank. For others, it might mean having enough residual income coming in monthly to completely cover your overhead. For example, if it's $5,000 per month that you're looking for, working in your existing job and going for a raise in pay might suffice. However, if $100,000 per month is what you intend to achieve, other alternatives such as starting your own business, investing in properties, or working on your "skill sets" to better serve the marketplace will probably be more effective. More importantly, knowing how much you want prepares your mind for the potential issues you may face to make that happen.

The challenge therefore becomes: How do you know how much you want? Arbitrarily quoting a figure will probably do you more harm than good. If the amount you pull out of the sky is much higher than what you really want, your approach to acquire the wealth may not be in harmony with your "why" and you may end up burning yourself out. In the event that the amount is lesser than what you really want, then you'll find yourself re-adjusting your "why," which may not inspire you to keep going. Again your "what," your "why," and your "mindset" need to be in harmony.

Determining how much you want doesn't have to be rocket science. You can do this by taking into consideration the objective for what you want the wealth for—your "why"—and do an analysis of the costs necessary to sustain it. Let's say for example that your reason is to provide your family with a comfortable lifestyle which includes overseas travel for vacations twice a year along with being debt free. You can include the costs of paying off your debt, traveling overseas for holiday twice a year, and your comfortable living expenses into your analysis.

A lot of people think having a wealthy mindset involves only constantly thinking about getting rich. That's not it at all. The most important element is to make the decision and after that not to obsess about how to do it. Take action and allow it to unfold. Play the "what if" game. Brainstorm possibilities. Be open to solutions. Expose your mind to possibilities…to new opportunities. Let go of your fears. Discuss with a qualified mentor or coach.

Suppose you want to get from point "A" to point "B." There's route 1, route 2, route 3, all the way to infinity. When you believe that there's only one way to get there, it limits your possibilities. When you are totally open to how to get there, the mind starts considering the many options and may prompt you to act on one of them that you haven't even thought of before. Along the way, your wealthy mindset may allow you to recognize different opportunities, encouraging you to change course and go through a totally different experience than originally planned.

I remember one man I knew about that attained wealth in a totally different manner than expected. Initially, his plan was to market his own music compositions through conventional methods. But he instead stumbled upon online internet marketing and embarked on an unconventional route to becoming an internet millionaire. It was not an easy route, as he had to juggle learning about the new internet marketing model of which he knew nothing about while still working a full-time job. But his burning desire to be rich got him through the hurdle to financial freedom.

Start to imagine yourself as already having wealth. Before you physically acquire the wealth that you've envisioned, you need to own it as if you already possess the amount of money that you desire! How would you feel right now if you were wealthy? What would you be doing differently? How would your life be different? How would your day unfold? Start to "own" the result of your wealth now! The subconscious mind is unable to differentiate between actual possession and mere visualization. So by imagining that you already have it, you're encouraging your subconscious mind to seek ways to transform your imaginary feelings into the real thing.

I know many people refute this type of thinking as impractical. But if you think about it, isn't everything around us a true manifestation of someone else's imagination? Everything man made was in someone's imagination before it was created. And when they possessed the passion to create it, the ways and means appeared. The Wright brothers imagined being able to fly and the reality is that we are now able to fly in an airplane from one country to another in a matter of hours. Thomas Edison imagined lighting the whole room using a single source and as a result, the lightbulb was invented! Yes, it took a few tries, about 10,000, but eventually he created it.

Look around right now. If you are in a room, look at all the things in that room that made someone wealthy. Why not you? Take a walk outside and look around. How many things do you see that made someone else wealthy? Why not you? It all started in someone's imagination. They owned it first in their mind before it became a reality. It's a fact that without the imagination of great visionaries, we would not be able to enjoy many things that we enjoy today. Radio, television, automobiles, and thousands of other great inventions we would not enjoy today if not for someone first imagining it into existence. Vision comes first, then the answers!

You too possess the same capability to create and improve your own destiny by constructing it in your mind first. All improvement in your life begins in the improvement of your mental pictures. Change your mental pictures and you change the outcome of your life, like changing a movie in a DVD player.

So how do you build this imagination? Jack Nicklaus calls it "going to the movies"; that's easy and fun to apply. He's known in the industry to have a very clear picture of how he should play the game before actually going into one. He visualizes an outcome before starting the game. He sees himself winning! In his own words, he states "I never hit a shot, not even in practice, without having a very sharp, in-focus picture of it in my head first. First I see the ball where I want it to fall, nice and white and sitting up high, easy to hit, on the green grass. Then the scene quickly changes, and I see the ball going there; its path, trajectory, and shape, and even how it lands. Then there is a sort of fade-out and the next scene shows me making the kind of swing that will turn the previous images into reality." You and I can do the same. For example, you can imagine receiving income checks when you open the mailbox every day. Or you can picture yourself receiving an award for being nominated the best entrepreneur in your country or having a best-selling book. Not only does it send the message to your subconscious, it serves as a great form of daily inspiration.

Okay, let's come in for a landing ...

It is absolutely essential to have a crystal-clear picture of what you want to accomplish before you begin. If you want to attain wealth, you must learn to operate with a sharply defined mental image of the outcome you want to attain.

Focus your attention on the spot where you want to land, not on where you are now, or on any misconceptions or shortcomings you may think you have. In other words, visualize your arrival and you'll develop a magnetic harmony with the ways and means required to get there. With a clear mental image, you'll attract the people and circumstances needed to get you where you want to go. Solutions will begin to appear and obstacles will seem to disappear. Answers will come to you. People will show up to support you in your endeavor. Look at the end result as something that you are already prepared to do; you just haven't done it yet.

You have the potential, and the resources are available for you to have anything you want. The only thing missing is your firm, unshakable decision, the wealth mindset, and letting go of your old way of thinking and believing.

Think about this. Your success is something that you have been preventing; it's not something you have to struggle to make happen. You can't force anything into existence. All you can do is step out of the way and let it unfold. The critical key is to not let fear, doubt, other people, or mind chatter push your success away.

The Change[10]

You'll find the solutions taking you toward your goals will come to you in the most unexpected and sudden ways when you let go of the old you and embrace the new you.

You don't need the *perfect* plan first. What you need is a *perfectly* clear decision about your success and the right mindset, and the ideal way to get you there will materialize. You can't get all the answers upfront, so don't waste your time trying.

The success formula doesn't involve getting everything neatly organized, with everything in its proper place and sequence and all the risks eliminated before you make the move. If you want that, then get a 9-5 job, but realize that will never make you wealthy.

If you want to be a wealthy entrepreneur, you have to sometimes shoot from the hip, going into new territory and charting the map as you go. Be willing to cope with confusion for a while and shape your plan as you go. Allow some disorder, and then create order out of it. If you get too detailed in the beginning, you'll find yourself worrying over potential problems and non-productive details, instead of what's really important, which is getting the job done. Get a target…point, then take action!

Your true greatness lies within your ability to decide what you want and your commitment to having it, and then taking bold action to get it. Develop your mindset and then imagine it into existence.

You've heard the saying "think outside the box!" Here's my version… "don't ever get in the box!" The world you have perceived in the past is the world you now live in. The world you perceive now is the world you will create in the future. And the world you create is limited only by your imagination, your mindset, and your ability to let go of the old you. Create your vision and then stand back and allow your conviction to decide the quality of your life and your degree of wealth!

Everyone has the right to be wealthy. You have the right to be wealthy. Yet, most allow a temporary lack of money to eat into their minds, literally confining them into the vicious cycle of mediocrity.

The bottom line is that people are poor because they have not yet decided to be rich. So long as you manage a conscious decision to become wealthy and have the utmost faith that you can achieve it, you will act accordingly to what you believe. We all create our own reality, abundant or not. A person who believes that the universe is abundant and they can attain whatever level of financial success they desire…and a person who believes that money only comes from working hard and will receive money only from hard work…are both right. Each will have many experiences to prove that their "belief" about abundance is a "fact."

The good news is…you can change your belief and therefore change what you experience.

www.JimBritt.com

www.PowerOfLettingGo.com

www.CrackingTheRichCode.com

www.FaceBook.com/JimBrittOnline

www.JourneyBeginsNow.com

Jim Lutes

Having taught his branded form of human performance since the early 1990s, Mr. Lutes has accelerated top-level entrepreneurs throughout his career by conducting trainings on personal growth and subconscious programming into worldwide markets.

During this time, Jim took his skills regarding the human mind, and combining it with trainings on influence, persuasion, and communication strategies, he launched Lutes International in the early 1990s. Based in San Diego, California, Jim has taught seminars for corporations, sales forces, individuals, and athletes. Having appeared on television, radio, and worldwide stages, Jim's style, knowledge, and effectiveness provide profound results.

"Jim Lutes possesses a unique ability to create performance change in an individual in a fraction of the time it takes his competitors." The core of human decisions are based on the programs we acquire, reinforce, and grow. Combining Jim's various trainings, individuals can reach new levels of achievement and fulfillment in all areas of life. The results are at times nothing short of astonishing.

It's Not Where You Are, It's Where You're Going

By Jim Lutes

When we realize we yearn for change in our lives, at the beginning it can feel like we will be forever trapped in who we were or used to be. Indeed, the past is highly influential in our present life, whether we are aware of it or not. Past experiences inform all kinds of decisions we make in a day, some of which we make without thinking. When you decide to enter into a new relationship with someone, your past experiences may make you wary or afraid of being hurt. When you create a new piece of music or a piece of art, past experiences of how your creativity has been received will inform how you go about presenting that piece. When you really want to start to make change, first you have to allow yourself to be free of the past.

Consider: It's not where you are right now, but where you're going, and let this be among the primary motivators in getting you to take the necessary steps to change. This means looking forward, not looking back. Looking forward to who you want to be, not looking only at who you are right in this moment. It is a fine line to dance on, but being able to see the potential of who you are and how it can evolve as you decide to change your life is what will get you to a place of achieving your goals and desires.

Let me share with you two of the most motivating emotional states for creating change and success. These are inspiration and desperation. Desperation can be a good thing because until you get really dissatisfied, you won't do anything to take your life to another level. Dissatisfaction, then, is actually awesome! And dissatisfaction is an opportunity to turn struggle into something else. If you are feeling completely satisfied, you will become comfortable. When we feel comfortable, we are unlikely to make changes in our lives. Then life begins to deteriorate.

After all, it is not what you accomplish in relation to others that is important, it's what you accomplish in relationship to your own potential. Your tomorrow is based on your today, and once you realize that the ability to create your brightest tomorrow is already within you, you will start moving in the best direction for yourself, the direction of change for the better. You will move into an empowered place in the course of your own life.

Your brain is the most powerful computer on the planet. When you learn to use it properly, you can create any result you want. Your brain can give you the answer to almost any problem you have. The problem is that this computer we call our brain is not user-friendly, and does not come with an owner's manual. This book will show you how to operate your supercomputer with precision. Lasting change is not created in your life by learning more. Lasting change is created by dissolving the emotions, thoughts, patterns, beliefs, and programming that simply no longer serve you, in order to allow yourself to truly tap into your connection with Universal Power. You must re-design your blueprint to create the kind of results you want in your life.

This is the basis of the work I am inviting you to do with this book. Today, you are beginning a process that can truly change the quality of your life forever and can take that paint-by-numbers life you might be living now and create the masterpiece called your life. So just for a moment now, what I want you to do is imagine that your life is a painting. Imagine that you have died and are looking down at that painting. What did you leave behind? Is your life a masterpiece that is cherished and hangs prominently as an example for others of what is possible, or is it a paint-by-numbers life that is packed away in someone's basement?

Where you are in your life right now is the direct result of making decisions unconsciously, stuck in patterns and beliefs that served you once, but have not evolved to continue to serve you now, as an adult. If you feel stuck or are not pleased with your circumstances, being aware of the choices you make—choices that come from someplace other than your conscious thoughts—is step number one to taking control of your life. If you feel great about your life, you can also benefit from this work, as there are still doubtless limiting beliefs and thoughts in your subconscious mind that affect you too, whether you realize it or not.

It's not about where you are; it's about where you're going. If you want to change your life and align all major aspects of your life—finances, health, relationships, emotional well-being—then looking at what shaped you, and stepping out of a limiting identity, is what will help you to make the changes you seek. In other words, you must become the kind of person who holds and embodies the characteristics and qualities that you value. Visualizing it, affirming it, and even living your life by a new set of standards is not going to work long-term until this stuff goes from your conscious to your subconscious and finally into your heart. Not only do you have to DO it, and not only do you have to LIVE it, you also have to BECOME it. Then, you will manifest it.

For us to really live consciously, to be an example for others, then we have to be aware of what is shaping us. Be aware of what programs your subconscious mind is already running, be aware of how the conscious and subconscious mind work together, and be aware of the thoughts you think that are disempowering, and how you can change those thoughts to empowering ones.

It is always amazing to me how people take more time in a day to pick out what they are going to watch on television than on programming their minds. We spend more time choosing what kind of products we're going to use to clean our bodies than considering how we are going to clean our minds! We put so much emphasis on the external, when the reality is that the external is driven by the internal. If you want success in money, relationships, health, and emotional health, you must start to work from the inside out.

It all comes down to the power of your mind, and this includes both your conscious and subconscious mind. You have in your power the ability to transform your thoughts into your allies or your adversaries. You are creating your day through the thoughts you think. The subconscious mind is a direct connection to Universal Power, or source, or whatever higher power there is for you. The subconscious mind responds to images and emotions that come to your mind through your thoughts. You have in your life exactly what you tell yourself you want; that is, if you are frustrated, you're telling yourself you're frustrated. If you're saying "I'm sick," then you are not enjoying good health. Our internal communication is the dialogue we have with ourselves each day, and it is mostly filled with old programming. This is how our subconscious minds work, without our even being aware of how they are working behind the scenes to sabotage us. Our internal communication perpetuates the realization of what we expect.

If your internal communication is laden with limiting beliefs, or running on patterns that have been held in your subconscious for your whole life, then you will not be able to live to your fullest potential. Your patterns of thought and beliefs that no longer serve you must be sacrificed if you want to align all elements of your life. When I say "It's not where you are, it's where you're going," this is what I'm talking about. Where you are right now, as you read this, continues to be the self that is held hostage by an identity formed when you were a child. You are being held hostage by the patterns your subconscious mind is running in the background of your every waking moment. Until you reprogram your subconscious mind to make conscious choices in place of these choices made out of habit, you will not be able to move yourself out of where you might feel stuck and into where you will prosper. I'm not just talking about prospering financially either! I'm talking about prospering in whatever area you want to prosper—health, relationships, emotional well-being, sure, finances too. The big picture "prosper"—another word for it is thrive. To move from surviving to thriving means moving forward into where you're going, and not staying settled into where you are.

Take stock of where you are right now, and start to see where you can bridge the gap between where you are, and where you want to go. Where you are going in your life depends upon the choices you make today. Picking up this book was one choice you made that can serve you as you step forward more fully into your life. Eating a donut mindlessly on your drive home from work was one choice that may have been completely unconscious, one that may have served your eight-year-old self, starving for love from your mother, but one that doesn't serve your vision of being fit and strong. (Note that occasionally indulging in a donut is ok, but making it a habit or doing it without thinking is not supporting your health goals.) By setting the intention to change, and deciding to make choices with awareness, through building smart connection between the subconscious and conscious minds, moment to moment, you will have a direct impact on each tomorrow as you build the future that you seek.

A close and careful read of this book is a unique opportunity to look deep inside yourself. Take a good look inside of your relationships, your decisions about money, and your decisions about your career, your relationship with the universe, or your higher power, and even your body. You will begin to understand how your own upbringing has influenced you and start identifying some of the decisions and habits you have created, including pinpointing one core decision that has affected your identity. Get clear about what really stands in your way (hint: it's you!).

Shifting your focus to become to become the kind of person you want to be has everything to do with YOU. If you want to change any circumstance or any relationship in your life, then you must begin with yourself, no matter how convinced you are that something else or somebody else must change. This is where we begin to shift from blaming others for our circumstances and recognizing our own internal sense of agency and power in building and sustaining the life of our dreams. Recognizing the patterns and habits that keep you in a place of "smallness" and fear is the first step. Then, as you begin to make shifts and changes, you will find yourself able to change even the most rigid system and stubborn person. I have experienced this myself. Every small change and shift is progress, and this moves you forward. Any movement forward, as a result of your desire and courage to make lasting changes, creates the opportunity for every other part of your life to be moved forward as well. Everything is interrelated, especially the parts of our lives that comprise the whole of our lived existence.

The past may have a hold on your present; indeed, it is a tricky one to extricate yourself from. However, you don't need to let it sit in the driver's seat. Taking control of your life and keeping a clear eye on the path ahead is one way of stepping out of the entanglement of the past. Use what you have learned, of course, but leave all that which is unnecessary. They call it "baggage" for a reason! Where you are right now is the starting point for where you're going. It is okay, nay, even necessary, to imagine yourself as who you want to be, and to let these imaginings trump any more carryover of feelings associated with who you were. It's not where you are or were, but where you're going that matters when you begin the journey of reprogramming your subconscious mind.

***

To contact Jim:

Email: info@lutesinternational.com

Websites: www.lutesinternational.com

www.jimluteslive.com

Julia A. Nicholson

For the past 20 years, Julia A. Nicholson has been inspiring thousands of board members, corporate executives, employees, and colleagues across the country to learn more and do more to be the best they can be. Julia's high energy draws people in and her success in overcoming significant tragedy and loss has inspired many, especially those facing situations and challenges that seemed insurmountable, giving them renewed hope. She has the unique ability to transfer her energy to others, while helping them identify actionable steps to move forward. She is passionate and committed to making a difference in the lives of others and can help you unlock your power and change your life!

In addition to her speeches and seminars, Julia has simultaneously been the CEO and Vice President/COO of multibillion dollar corporations for the past 16 years. She successfully balanced the competing demands of being a single parent, earning multiple college degrees, and running complex, dynamic corporations by continually practicing her life lessons. Julia graduated summa cum laude from the University of Missouri with Bachelor of Science degrees in Business Administration – Finance and Management and Organizational Behavior and earned her MBA from the University of Denver.

The Moment Everything Changes

By Julia A. Nicholson

As we piled into the car that night heading to the lake, with my sister in the backseat and me in the front passenger seat, we talked non-stop, wanting to make the most of our time together. I hadn't seen her since she moved 800 miles away and I really missed her. After looking at her in the backseat, I turned back around just in time to see the headlights hurling toward us on the deserted two-lane highway. The drunk driver hit us head-on at a high rate of speed, crushing the front end and side of the car around me, trapping me in the front passenger seat with the dashboard at my chest and the firewall at my feet, unconscious, severely injured, and losing blood quickly. While unconscious, I saw things I had never seen before and the faces of people I loved flashed rapidly in my mind. *This must be what it's like to be dead*, I thought. Everyone who had materialized on the side of the road to offer assistance had the same grave opinion of my condition, as did my sister. Only God, with a perfectly timed series of miracles, including a penny that lodged in my seatbelt at precisely the exact moment it was needed, could have saved my life that night.

I knew my injuries were bad, but I didn't know how bad until I saw the tears in my father's eyes the first time he saw me after the accident. Three tours in Vietnam did not prepare my father, a career Marine, to see his 18-year-old daughter so battered. That is when I began to understand just how horrific my injuries were. Reflective surfaces were kept away as I had significant facial trauma. My entire top jaw bone had been shattered and my face was so swollen I could see the entire bottom half of my face just by casting my eyes downward. When I was stable enough to fly home, people gasped and pointed at me like I was something out of a horror movie as I walked to my gate in the Dallas/Ft. Worth airport.

Back at my parents' home, I declined almost all calls and all visitors. Enduring countless medical appointments and multiple surgeries, my physical injuries began to heal. It was the unseen emotional and mental toll of my injuries with which I struggled. At 18 years old, that night's event had destroyed my self-confidence, self-esteem, and self-worth. I went from being a happy, energetic, active, optimistic, outgoing person to an isolated, depressed, pessimistic, lifeless one who didn't fit in the world anymore. I isolated myself from just about everyone and everything for months. I wanted to crawl into a cave and die. Please, no more doctors, surgeons, dentists, orthodontists, endodontists….no more reopening wounds, prodding, poking, x-raying, cutting, stitching, questioning, staring, gasping, pointing…I just wanted to be left alone. I sank further and further into a black hole. Months went by and all I could think of was "why me?" Why me? I didn't do anything wrong. I didn't knowingly make a bad choice. I didn't deserve this. I was a victim of circumstance and through no fault of my own, tragically my life was ruined. I had always had a very strong faith in God, but I was empty now and felt nothing.

One morning after months of languishing in a physical and mental hell, I woke up and my question had changed. Instead of "why me?" the question "Why NOT me?" was pounding in my head. Why would I wish this on anyone else? Why would I want anyone else to go through this trauma? Why should someone else suffer? It was at this moment everything changed. I knew God had given me a second chance at life and I started pondering how blessed I was to still be alive and the incredible series of miracles that occurred to save my life—like the make of the car I was in, the height of the driver of our car, and the penny in my seatbelt buckle. As I recalled the story about the single set of footprints in the sand, I knew I had been carried through this time by grace. Then more questions came. What am I supposed to learn from the entire experience? How can I use the experience to become a better person? What am I supposed to do now that I have been given a second chance? Can I use my experience to help someone else?

With this new perspective, I mistakenly thought I was "healed" and ready to jump back into life. I had no clue that it would take much longer for the mental and emotional damage to heal. The lack of understanding my mental and emotional state put me in a marriage less than 2 years after the accident to the first man who showed me some attention. That marriage turned out to be just as devastating as the drunk driver.

5 years later...

With my hand still on the cold metal door knob of our baby's bedroom door after putting her down for the night, I heard him walking up the stairs. As I turned, I saw him coming down the hall at me with the same look in his eyes that I had seen countless times before. He was enraged again, for some unknown reason. It was the same look that always made my heart race with fear as I cringed and became apologetic and submissive, trying to calm him down before he lashed out. I feared for my children. As I stood there, I realized that I was just waiting for his wrath to be spent on me again. Would it be verbal, emotional, or physical this time? How long would it last? How bad would it be? As thoughts of our two young daughters crossed my mind, something in me snapped. It was at this moment everything changed. This time I didn't cringe and I didn't retreat. This time I met his enraged, domineering glare with my own. An overwhelming force unlike any I had ever known overcame me. Standing in front of our baby's bedroom door, looking straight into his eyes, with more power, strength, and conviction than I had ever experienced or exhibited before, I loudly, forcefully, and defiantly declared, "THAT'S IT. I'VE HAD IT. I will NEVER be in this situation again as long as I live." I had no idea the profound difference that changing my thinking and verbalizing my thoughts would make until much later.

He must have sensed something had dramatically changed in that moment too, because this time he froze right where he was. Almost instantaneously, he went from being enraged and threatening to warm, apologetic, and conciliatory. His face softened and his body language changed to that of a sad, scolded child. It was too late; it didn't matter. In that instant, nothing mattered, except getting myself and my two daughters out of there, which is exactly what I did.

Until that moment, I had felt stuck, trapped, imprisoned by my own choices, and perhaps worst of all, hopeless and helpless to do anything about it. All my thoughts were about what I didn't have, what I couldn't do, the insurmountable obstacles I would face if I tried to leave, the negative opinions people would have about me if I was divorced, and I was convinced that there was no way I could make it on my own. I had no job, no training or education other than a high school diploma, no money, no savings, and no way to support myself or my children. With my already low self-confidence and self-esteem, which was further eroded by his 5 years of abuse and constant reminders that I was stupid, useless, weak, worthless, ugly, and that I'd never amount to anything, I believed I had no other choice but to stay in the marriage.

The stress of the marriage had taken a toll on my physical health as well. At 23 years old, I had such debilitating joint pain and limited mobility in my hands that it was extremely painful to do anything including picking up or holding my baby or changing her diaper. The rheumatologist who examined me said I had all the symptoms of an 80 year-old with severe rheumatoid arthritis. The stress was taking such a toll on my body that if I didn't resolve it, I would require gold shots, a last-resort treatment for pain relief, before I was 30.

A Thought Can Change Everything!

What happened to propel me from my depressed, despondent, "why me" state after my car accident to an introspective, reflective "why not me" state? What happened that I went from lacking self-confidence, self-esteem, and self-worth, feeling helpless in an unbearable marriage to subsequently being able to raise two incredible daughters, work three jobs simultaneously to pay the bills, earn a real estate license, graduate summa cum laude with two bachelor degrees, earn an MBA, become a nationally sought after speaker and instructor, and be in my first CEO position of a $450M company just 12 years later? Given the numerous challenges and obstacles I encountered along the way, how were any of these accomplishments possible for a single mother of two who was raised by a father who never graduated from high school and a mother who believed strongly that a good mother stayed home and took care of her family?

As I reflected on my journey, trying to answer these questions, I realized none of the facts changed regarding any situation or obstacle I faced. I still had the same physical injuries from the accident, the same self-confidence, self-esteem, and self-worth issues, the same problems in my marriage, the same lack of education, and the same financial issues with no money to support myself or my children. I didn't suddenly have a miraculous recovery, a healthy, supportive marriage, or become formally educated or wealthy.

No matter what else I tried to attribute any turning point in my life to, it always came back to the same thing. Each turning point occurred the moment the way I thought about the situation changed. Changing my thoughts and being able to see the situation differently were the first and most important steps to accomplishing everything I have accomplished. Changing what I thought led to changing what I believed was possible. Overcoming the challenges and achieving so much in such a short period of time were only possible when my thoughts changed, and then everything else followed—the things I was telling myself, how I viewed the situation, how I felt physically, mentally, and emotionally, the options I had available to me, what I believed was possible, and finally my actions. I slowly began to realize and accept that it was the negative, pessimistic, self-defeatist, limiting <u>thoughts that I believed</u> that had really trapped me, made me fearful, and held me hostage.

What an epiphany! My thoughts are something I could have control over and I didn't need a job, money, or formal education to do it! I had a choice! I realized I had unconsciously let someone or something else control my thoughts and beliefs about myself, thereby controlling me. Just because I sustained visible injuries in a car accident didn't mean my life was ruined. Just because someone said I was dumb, worthless, no good, etc. didn't make any of those things true. Just because I didn't have a formal education didn't mean I couldn't make it on my own. These types of thoughts were only "true" as long as I believed they were true.

The concept of changing your thoughts and reasoning seems relatively simple on the surface; however, consciously and consistently controlling your thoughts is one of the most difficult things to do. When I did not consciously control my own thoughts, I was merely accepting the negative thoughts and opinions of others, thereby giving them control over me. To change my thoughts, I started to question what I thought and why. This led to significant changes in what I believed and my entire perspective in each situation changed. I started thinking about what was possible, instead of what was impossible. I started thinking about what I could do, instead of what I couldn't. I started thinking about what it would take to do "it"—whatever "it" was—instead of all the reasons why I couldn't do "it." I started thinking about the future, instead of beating myself up over the past. I started looking forward with hope, instead of backward with regret. This shift in thinking was empowering and energizing. Slowly, I started rebuilding "me" by consciously replacing the limiting, fear-based, negative thoughts with can-do-just-gotta-find-a way, hopeful, positive thoughts.

The process of rebuilding "me" and being able to overcome so many challenges and obstacles was not quick or easy. It included the confirmation of things I had heard many times: there is no free-ride, no substitute for hard work and determination, and no substitute for believing in yourself. If you want it, you must go after it. No one is going to give it to you. You must be committed to what you want and be willing to work for it. When you get knocked down, you have to get back up again. Be willing to accept help—no one does it all on their own. And no matter what, don't ever lose sight of what's really important to you.

My path included many periods of doubt, frustration, discouragement, heartache, and tears, as well as countless setbacks and sacrifices; however, without all of the trials and tribulations I encountered, I wouldn't be who I am today. Facing and overcoming these allowed me to learn who I really am and what I'm made of. My journey has also given me some invaluable skills and taught me critical life lessons that I rely on every day. I attribute my accomplishments and continued success to learning and continually practicing the following life lessons:

Control your thoughts! Be conscious of your thoughts and control them intentionally or they will control you unconsciously. Don't give someone or something else control over your thoughts or emotions. Actively stop negative thoughts by asking yourself "Is there another way to view this? Do I really believe this? Do I really want to feel this way?" and replace them with positive thoughts. There is always more than one way to view anything. Realize that your thoughts can help you or hurt you, propel you or drain you, motivate you or demoralize you…so make sure your thoughts are building you up, inspiring you, and energizing you.

Stay focused! Don't let anything derail you—especially the opinions of others, even if they are close to you. Be deliberate with your actions. Stay committed. Avoid physical, mental, and emotional vampires that will suck the life out of you. Ignore the naysayers. Keep a journal or make a list of all the reasons why you are doing what you are doing and what caused you to make a change. It will be invaluable to keep you on track when you start to doubt yourself and why you are doing what you are doing. Above all, don't ever lose sight of what really matters to you.

You always have choices! Take responsibility for your current situation. Your choices, conscious or not, are why you are where you are today. You may not like any of the choices you have, or you may be afraid to make a choice, but you always have a choice. Doing nothing is a choice. Sometimes you have to make tough choices. If fear is paralyzing you, identify what you are afraid of and why and then realize the exact opposite outcome is also a possibility. For instance, if you are afraid to leave a job because you might not find another one, also think about the possible outcome of finding an even better job because you left your current one. Remember that fear is only created by our thoughts. Fear doesn't necessarily prevent a mistake or an accident. Many times, fear only prevents you from living life. Remember one of the most important choices you make is how you choose to perceive something.

Look forward! Don't dwell on the past and don't look back, unless it will help move you forward. Looking backward only drains your energy and tends to pull you backward physically, mentally, and emotionally—you must be thinking and looking forward to move forward. It is impossible to achieve your future goals by continually looking backward and focusing on the past.

Set Your Own Bar! Don't do anything to prove something to anyone else and don't use anyone else's bar for you as a measurement of yourself. If you use someone else's bar, the bar always changes when the "someone" whose approval you are seeking changes. Not only is this exhausting and setting yourself up for failure, since there will always be multiple bars all the time (i.e., your mother, father, significant other, sibling, boss, child, friend, co-worker, etc.), it is impossible to continually meet a changing bar. Do whatever you are doing for you and set your own bar for yourself!

Be true to yourself, kind to yourself, and believe in yourself! Your foundational beliefs, ethics, and integrity should not be for sale. You must take care of yourself and believe in yourself before anyone else will.

Express gratitude! No one is successful on their own. Acknowledge the help, support, and encouragement you have received. There is always something to be grateful and thankful for…find it and acknowledge it. Celebrate the little wins. It will help you to keep moving forward.

Know that controlling your thoughts is something you must do continually. You will never be "done," as there will always be more negative thoughts trying to set up residence in your mind. Every person has a tipping point—where "it" is so uncomfortable, so unbearable, and so untenable that anything is better than your current situation. This is the critical point when you either break and lose more of yourself, or you change your thinking, which changes your beliefs and actions and you become more than you ever imagined possible. The choice is yours.

You will know when you are ready to change your thinking when most of your thoughts are about how you can make "it" work, instead of all the reasons why "it" won't. If your thoughts are primarily about why "it" won't work, you aren't quite ready yet and you have a little more work to do, but you will get there if you are committed and stay focused!

If you are faced with situations and challenges that seem insurmountable, know and embrace the truth—your own thoughts are holding you back. Start changing your life by changing your thoughts! You can either make excuses or make progress, but you can't do both at the same time. As long as you are making excuses, it is impossible for you to make progress. Believe in you and take charge of the Business of You, Inc.! Stay tuned—there's more Business of You, Inc. to come!

***

To Contact Julia:

www.JuliaANicholson.com

www.BusinessOfYouInc.com

www.JNicholsonConsulting.com

Email: Julia@JuliaANicholson.com

Beth Haley

I take great joy in the positive feedback I get from clients about the positive shifts that they are able to make in their lives as a result of putting into practice the suggestions I offer them and as they learn to use the tools that I share with them. As an entrepreneur, coach, mentor, wife, mother, and grandmother, my approach to coaching tends to be a nurturing one. My focus is on assisting my clients with a sense of well-being, self-empowerment, and healing of long-standing wounds. As clients heal from past emotional hurts and learn mechanisms to cope and then flourish, their lives change! My clients have enjoyed results ranging from beneficial changes in their personal lives, healthier relationships with loved ones, emotional triggers have been released, healthy thought patterns have been developed, solutions to sleeping difficulties, an increased ability to connect more clearly with their own intuition, release of phobias and fears, forgiveness related to long-held personal issues, women who have had self-esteem issues related to being sexually abused as children have healed their self-destructive patterns and replaced them with healthier patterns, and others have created constructive work environment changes as a result of personal sessions with me.

Change through Choice: Choosing to Create the Relationship You Want

By Beth Haley

You met your soul mate and things were perfect; but now it's been a while. You find yourself *wishing* that your relationship could be better. You have fantasies of being in the perfect relationship with your perfect partner, but you don't know how to get there.

How well does your current relationship measure up to your fantasies? Are you finding yourself in what seems to be a constant battle, bickering and fighting with your partner? Or do you have easy, loving communication with your partner? Do you find yourself making excuses not to be with your partner? Or do you look forward to the end of the day when you get to be with your partner? Do you find yourself imagining what life would be like if you were alone? Or is it impossible to imagine a future without your partner in it? If your relationship no longer looks like what you hoped it would be, know that you can change your experience by making 3 empowering choices.

Where do you start? Imagine your perfect relationship. What does that really look like to you? Imagine what your perfect partner is like, what your perfect partner would do, how your perfect partner would treat you. Now, include how you are being with your perfect partner, how you would be around that person, how you would treat that perfect someone. Visualize a clear, moving picture, *in color*, of what you want to create for yourself and your partner.

Visualizing a clear, moving picture of your perfect relationship helps your subconscious mind to know what you really desire so that it can help you to create just what you want. Your subconscious mind is that part of you that knows when to have your heart beat, when to blink, and thousands of other automatic processes. Wouldn't you like it to help you create a better relationship, too?

Being able to create your perfect relationship requires not only that your perfect partner be perfect for you, but for you to be the perfect partner for that person as well. Unfortunately, *perfect* is nearly next to impossible for anyone to be. In reality, a great relationship has perfect moments, but it is not perfect all the time. It's not very complicated to create lots of perfect moments. That's a relief, isn't it?

There are many components to having, or creating, a great relationship. Having been married now for over thirty-five years (to the same partner), I can tell you that there will be many shifts that will happen during the course of your relationship. Many of those shifts will not be smooth, or easy. With the right tools, you can handle the rough patches with a bit of grace, maybe even with joy. I certainly wish I had the information I am about to share sooner. My hope is that you and your relationship will benefit from reading this chapter. If you like what you read, I hope you consider making an appointment with me and allow me the privilege to assist you even further.

Choose every day to fall for your partner, over and over again.

Wouldn't it be great to wake up every morning and see the person you fell in love with and know that all of those great qualities you first saw in your partner are still there? That can be your reality, if you *choose* that reality. It will take some effort on your part, but choosing to see your partner through fresh eyes every day will add life to your relationship.

When you think of others making decisions for you or choices being imposed upon you, you are giving away your power. Knowing that YOU are making the choices in your life, even if it is something as simple as how you choose to see your partner, is very empowering.

Making the choice to nurture your relationship is not always easy, but it is rewarding. It is always interesting to me that, even after so many years together, my husband and I can still find something new about each other that surprises and delights both of us. Although most relationships are not usually boring, they can become quite comfortable and complacent.

After a number of years together, it is likely that your most intimate relationship is the one that gets ignored first. Have you become apathetic, assuming that your partner will always be there? Are you paying less attention and making it easier for your partner to put in less effort? All those amazing qualities you once found charming can get buried in the daily grind.

Choosing your partner again every day allows you to focus on all the wonderful things about your partner. You open a door to new possibilities when you create the space for your partner to be more perfect on a daily basis. What you think about, you bring about! When you focus on the good things; suddenly there are more of them. There is often a synchronicity at work that may or may not appear on the surface. Your thoughts are like magic. They draw more of what you think about into your life than you are aware of. Choose to keep your thoughts about your partner positive and loving. Then pay attention to how things start to change.

When you choose to ignore or not pay attention to your partner, you are in essence choosing to fail at the most profound opportunity you have in life to grow old with someone you love and who loves you in return. An intimate partner is someone that you can be totally yourself with. This gives you a wonderful opportunity to learn from each other, to smooth your own rough edges, and to grow in a multitude of ways. You get to choose, by how you are being, whether the growth environment is a good one or not. Loss of a relationship is often caused by a lack of growth, usually seen in a partner creating the same problem over and over again. Eventually, forgiveness is no longer an option, and the relationship self-destructs from there.

When you consider your partner and yourself in designing your relationship together, you can hold a powerful intention for your relationship. When you can hold that intention strongly enough, miracles can happen. When you see the world through the eyes of what you have in common with others, and when you act from a place of love, as opposed to reacting from a place of fear, you can move mountains. Are you able to look at all your similarities instead of all your differences? Can you work toward a common goal instead of being divisive?

The truth is, you already know that if you do not maintain your car or your home, it starts to fall apart. The same is true for your relationship. No matter how long you have been together, it is important to do your best to nurture the relationship. Remember when you noticed every little thing about your partner so you could figure out what would make them happy? Think of one thing you can do today for your partner that you haven't done for a while, and choose to DO IT. When you take another's needs into consideration and make decisions from a heartfelt point of view, you will realize the rewards and benefits in your relationship.

Choose to express yourself clearly, honesty, and lovingly when you communicate with your partner.

We all go into relationships with certain expectations, beliefs, and habits, some of which you may have developed as far back as early childhood. You have things you want to achieve and experience in partnership with someone you love. Some of those you are very aware of. Others may remain hidden. Do you know what your partner's expectations are of you, for the relationship? Do you know your own? These are important discussions and hopefully they happen early in a relationship. Have you reached a place where you each know what your goals in life are? Take the time to really get to know your partner and encourage them to get to know you, in a deep and meaningful way.

When we take the opportunities offered to us to form a lasting pair bond, we are letting ourselves in for major opportunities to learn how to get along with another. You are also given the opportunity to help your partner become a better, more well-rounded person when you help them see, through loving eyes, some changes that might help them to get past their own life challenges. This is not an excuse to pass judgement or criticize your partner. It is an opportunity to lovingly communicate with them how their unwanted behaviours are affecting you and perhaps others in their life. A loving partner will find ways to communicate that are not hurtful or blaming.

If you do not understand each other, or do not even have the desire to understand each other, the relationship starts to fall apart quickly. Effective communication involves both listening clearly and speaking clearly. Listening to you partner and making sure that what was expressed was interpreted properly is just as important as speaking to your partner and making sure that what you expressed was interpreted correctly.

People leave relationships every day though, because there are mistakes that have been made that have broken the relationship permanently for one partner or the other. There is usually no going back after a "deal breaker" mistake. If you hold back on letting your partner know what lines can't be crossed because you are afraid or want to keep the upper hand, that is not being loving. Open up and choose to talk with your partner about what your "deal breaker" issues are. Ask about theirs.

For a lot of people, fidelity is the number one deal breaker issue. Have you honestly expressed what fidelity means for you? Do you know how your partner defines fidelity? If not, it's time to discuss what your mutual expectations are around fidelity and how you both expect to interact with others. Don't let your relationship break because you each have different ideas about what being faithful means.

Arguments about money can be deal *crushers*. More than one relationship has faltered, or been lost, due to differences in financial goals and spending habits. Are your financial goals and habits compatible? Write your goals down, define what your needs are, and allow the opportunity to renegotiate with your partner as new situations come up.

If you haven't yet had a forthright conversation about whether or not to have children, don't delay. Honesty is critical when discussing family. Children are a lifetime commitment, and if you are not on the same page with this decision, your choice to continue with a relationship should be discussed. Make sure you are both in agreement and not expecting the other partner to "come around" or change their mind.

Many jokes are told about mothers-in-law, but how are you really going to handle extended family issues? No one can push your buttons harder than family. Don't let problems with caustic or unreasonable parents, siblings, or other extended family create havoc inside your primary family. Your relationship and any children are your primary family and all of your primary family needs must be considered as primary. Talk with each other about how to present a united front when extended family issues arise.

Relationships come in all kinds of different forms and there is no one right way to co-create a relationship. Developing your own tools and a communication style that works for both partners is something that takes time. When both sides know that they have been truly heard and feel understood, it is much easier to come to agreements and solve conflicts. In a situation where healthy communication thrives, you and your partner will be able to assist each other in recognizing belief patterns around the issues that arise. You can then help each other make the necessary changes that could help permanently alleviate the problem.

Choose to commit to being the best partner you can be in the relationship.

One of the great things about being in a relationship is the opportunity to see yourself and your habits through the eyes of someone who loves you. It gives you an amazing opportunity to grow and you will become a better person if you choose to learn how to smooth out the rough edges we all have.

Choose, every single day, to be the best partner that you can be. Choosing to be a true partner, in the fullest expression of what partnership means to you, means doing the best things possible for yourself and for your partner, every day. When you know that you are doing your best to foster a good relationship, any challenges or conflicts that arise become less stressful. We all make mistakes; that is part of being human. The key is in owning up to those errors in judgment, asking for forgiveness, and doing the best you can not to repeat them. It is totally up to your partner as to whether to forgive you, or not. Forgiveness cannot be demanded; it can only be requested. Requesting forgiveness often entails a commitment to not repeat the problem that created the situation in the first place.

When you feel truly happy about your role in maintaining the best relationship possible, you can let go of beating up on yourself. With a healthier, more positive attitude, you will probably find that your partner does not hold on to negative energy for very long, either. This creates a much more relaxed environment for fostering a good relationship.

Conversely, there may be times when your partner makes a mistake. Then it becomes your choice to hold on to the issue, or to forgive and move on. Holding on to mistakes only serves to keep them interfering in your present moments together and denies both of you the opportunity to move past the problem. It is truly a choice for your partnership when you can let go of past mistakes, practice forgiveness, and create an environment for a more loving relationship.

However, in the final analysis, as much as you might wish to be able to change your partner, in truth, you can only change yourself and how you choose to react to situations that are upsetting. It is in choosing how you will respond to a situation that you can exercise power over your situation. Understand that the choices you make and how you respond to situations that are uncomfortable to you is often more about you than about your partner.

The comfort zone you have gotten used to is seldom actually comfortable in the long run. When you avoid your responsibility to live life from a bigger place, or when you do not take responsibility for your own life by blaming others for your difficulties, you give away your power. Choosing a relationship from a place of self-determination is a much more powerful choice than clinging to a relationship from a place of feeling weak or needing support. If you have done the work to be the best person you can be, your partner can feel safe and be inspired to be the best person they can be. That's a big win for both of you, and the relationship.

Your perfect relationship awaits …

… all you have to do is find your vision and choose to follow it. Know that your limitations are only determined by your fears and your ego.

Holding a powerful vision for your relationship and for your life is the ultimate manifestation tool. There are many great people who did not have a great start in life. But they had a vision, and they did not let anyone knock them off their course of pursuing that vision. Martin Luther King did not live in a world that he liked, but he knew it could be changed. His vision of a better future actually brought that future into reality. Whatever state your relationship is in now, know that it can be changed. Spend some time every day visioneering the future of your relationship and watch how quickly you make it a reality.

Mother Theresa started out doing small acts of kindness, but as she held tight to her vision, she brought other people into her world and together they all changed the world. Choose to fall in love with your partner, today and every day. Commit small acts of kindness for your partner and watch the changes begin. See this as something you choose to do for yourself because you truly desire a deep and meaningful relationship. Choose to share the vision of your relationship with your partner and bring other people into your world who can help support you.

You can change your relationship by choosing to live your life from a place of purpose and power. Don't let anyone dissuade you from achieving, or at the very least, working on bringing your visions to life.

I truly hope that you have found the information in this chapter useful. If you choose it to be so, and are ready to do the work to make it happen, your current relationship can measure up to your fantasies. If you are having some challenges making new choices or if you require some assistance in removing blocks or fears that keep you from living the vision you want to hold, I would be very pleased to support you.

***

To Contact Beth:

Website: www.bethhaley.com

http://bethhaley.com/beth/#sthash.oFw4fuSo.dpuf

Call 403-973-8124 to book a coaching appointment.

If you would like to read more about building your relationship, I am currently finishing the book *88 Keys to Harmonious Relationships*, which will be coming soon.

David Heavener

As an eighteen year old, David Heavener moved to Nashville, where he penned two Top Ten Country hits and wrote for Johnny Carson and *Hee Haw*. In Hollywood, he became an award-winning filmmaker and actor with films on HBO, Showtime, USA, and worldwide television. David has starred with legends such as Tony Curtis and Martin Landau. His non-profit is producing an action/adventure feature film raising awareness on human trafficking. www.ChainedInnocence.com

David teaches his success formula in live and online acting, filmmaking, and entrepreneur workshops. David's soon to be released books *Lights, Camera, Take Action,* and *Power: A Spiritual Revolution,* contain principles vital to success and will be on his website, www.DavidHeavener.com.

Your Life is a Movie: Lights. Camera. *Take Action.*

By David Heavener

In my thirty years of writing and producing over forty films, I've directed and starred with top Hollywood legends like Tony Curtis, Martin Landau, Ernest Borgnine, and Oliver Reed, to name a few. I've applied certain techniques to my life that each of these stars brought to my set. I often wonder, "What makes these actors *great* actors?" The immediate answer seems obvious—they were *born* great actors. However, I work with other great actors, and few achieve what these stars accomplish. Most others never get very far at all. Why is that? The answer then became clear; and that is what I'll share with you. Each actor had three principles that launched their careers. These principles apply not only to acting, but also to any goal in life—personal, business, or even spiritual—and when personally realized, can launch anyone to the height of success. Be prepared, it can happen to you.

Roll the Cameras

Life is not an audition or a dress rehearsal. Life is more than a learning experience; it's thinking, planning, and *doing* experience. It is here and now. From the time you are born to the time you take your last breath, *life is the making of your movie.* You have locations, lights, cameras, actors, dialogue, makeup, wardrobe, props, extras, and you—*the star*. Perhaps you feel your lights and cameras have never been turned on, or your lights have been on and cameras rolling, but you are waiting for someone to call "Action." Maybe you're still memorizing your dialogue or touching up your makeup. You are trying to succeed, but time just keeps passing and nothing is happening. Martin Landau, my friend and co-star of *Eye of the Stranger,* said to me, "To *try* to do something is to *not* do it. It's a formula to fail." "Action" has already been called. The cameras are rolling. Your life is happening right now. You are living your screenplay this moment. Here's an excerpt from my book *Lights, Camera, Take Action* in which I describe three principles essential to the success of every film—and any goal in life. Let's touch on the first principle.

Principle #1 - Write It

It All Starts with the Script

Any good filmmaker or actor will tell you "It's all about the script." You can have a five hundred-million-dollar budget with top actors and an award-winning director, great camera people and editors, but without the script, you have nothing. Your life is like a script. No one can pen your story except you, through the victories and valleys of your life.

Writing your Script

Most people allow their script to be written by their family, friends, educational background, and circumstances. This, however, is not the intention of our Creator, who has given each of us the power, wisdom, and understanding to perfectly pen our own story. So how do we "write" our life? How do we know *what* to write? Here are three important points in order to stay on track throughout the writing process:

1. Passion

Passion is a term that has been thrown around by spiritual leaders and motivational mentors—but what is real passion? Real passion is the seed that lives in each of us. Before we are even born, the Sower plants the seed within us so it can take root and grow. This seed is as real as our vital organs and as important as the functions that keep us alive. Show me your passion and I'll show you your purpose. The world takes special interest in the care of our physical, mental, and spiritual wellness. Little is ever mentioned, however, about the "passion seed"—that tiny precious and unique gift in each and every one of us. Unfortunately, many people never nurture their seed, or worse yet, discover it. I believe this is the root cause of most diseases and many emotional and mental issues. Too much emphasis is placed on academics, money, and physical well-being, while the heart of who we really are dies. Passion is often traded for something we don't even like, or even at times believe in, such as our occupation or relationships. Our passion seed begins to go dormant because our God-given gifts and true purpose are not realized. Passion always strives toward perfection. I directed Robert Reed, the famous father of *The Brady Bunch* in his last film before he passed away. Even though he knew his condition was terminal, he played that scene as if it was the most important performance of his life. He looked tired on the set, so I told him he didn't have to work so hard. I'll never forget what he said: "When you have a passion for something, perfection should always be the goal." Indeed, the very goal of this book is to help revive your seed and allow it to grow to its full potential, giving birth to your purpose.

2. Power

When purpose is discovered and the passion seed is in full bloom, an interesting thing happens inside your soul. It's called Full Power Consciousness. Full Power Consciousness is born when we know exactly what the Creator intends for us to be. When we obtain Full Power Consciousness, we possess the exact ingredient that lifts us to the height of success. It's a state of mind (but also emotion and spirit); a place of peace with our Creator. We *know* that we know. We are centered and possess a glimpse of infinite wisdom. We understand that success is at our door and all we need to do is open up. Full Power Consciousness propels the passion seed to the finish line of championship. It always hits its mark. When we carry Full Power Consciousness, it's possible to be healthy and spiritually enlightened. How can we obtain it? One day on the set of *Prime Target*, I asked Tony Curtis, "What does it take to become a star?" He replied, "You don't *become* a star. You just *are*." He meant that first we must believe. Belief is faith—faith in the knowledge that you are uniquely created by love for love. That's the fuel to jumpstart Full Power Consciousness. Jesus says, "Your faith has made you whole." "Whole" means complete, in perfect condition, integrated in thought, words, and action. Wholeness is where our thoughts match our words and through power, our words turn into action.

3. Prosperity

Prosperity is a word that has been misused in association with money, things, or position. True prosperity really means to grow, expand, and to rise above. This could mean financially, but more importantly, it means spiritually, emotionally, and mentally. People tend to attach money to prosperity because of the illusion that money can buy anything. Money is just an extension of a person and usually amplifies their most predominant thoughts and characteristics. For example, if someone with money is dishonest, chances are their money will be used to obtain more money dishonestly. On the other hand, if a person is generous, then they will usually be generous with their money. If a person does not respect money, then it generally flees. I met a lottery winner who won millions only to find out that just eighteen months later, she had spent every last penny and was broke. Money is a tool to be used with wisdom and understanding to promote our purpose. Now let's get back to our three principles.

Principle #2 - Shoot It

Life Offers No Rehearsals

Many times, I direct my camera crew to "shoot the rehearsal," which means that they are to turn on the lights and camera while the actors are rehearsing. Why? First, I usually receive a better performance from actors during rehearsal, simply because the pressure is off. Second, sometimes I'm running behind schedule and need to make up for lost time. Both of these scenarios may also be true in life. Our rehearsal is our performance. Everything we think, feel, say, and do is the performance. Not every performance will be stellar; but this does not mean we focus on what we call failures or inadequacies, or convince ourselves that our past is who we are now. Time is something we can never reclaim. We should always approach life as if we are behind schedule, not in a negative way, but in a way that keeps us on our toes in completing the mission assigned to us. Each of us is a product of heredity, environment, circumstances, and a belief system, which together produce the movie of our life. Let's look at these in detail:

Heredity

People say, "He inherited his father's bad temper" or "Her mother passed on that alcohol addiction to her daughter." The truth is, what we inherit from our parents has little to do with our physiological outcome. Of course, the color of our hair or eyes most often reflects our parents; however, genes play only a small role.

Environment

"She's a product of her environment." Nice try, but no cigar. Does a poor, or rich, or in-between environment dictate a person's outcome? The answer is, only if they let it. There are many stories of children who grow up in pee-poor neighborhoods and attend horrible schools only to become very successful in life. Likewise, there are rich kids who turn out to be complete losers. The fact is, environment does not have to determine whom we become, other than to build character and enhance spiritual understanding if we allow.

Circumstances

It's true that certain negative situations can leave scars, just as positive events can build character. If we choose to let our scars start new wars, we will just stay on the battlefield of hurt and self-pity in a victim mentality. Circumstances and events are just that—circumstances are a chain of events—and events occur at a point in time lasting only a period of time. Events can be canceled and circumstances can be changed.

Our Belief System

Scripture tells us to guard our thoughts because as a person thinks, so he is. Our belief system is the most powerful aspect of who we are because it sculpts our reality on a moment-by-moment basis. Tell me what you focus on and I'll tell you what rules your life. Is it fear, negativity, and hatred or love, happiness, and helping others? Or maybe it's money, career, and getting ahead. If we believe we amount to nothing and are doomed for failure, then guess what? We are. If we believe that our Creator constantly judges us and is waiting for us to mess up, then we stand judged. If we believe that we are truly loved and successful in spite of our circumstances, then we are. Fortunately, we can change our belief system and therefore change our destiny.

Hit your mark

When an actor is directed to move on the set, a "mark" is placed on the floor so they know where to move. The mark is vital because if the actor does not hit their mark, the director is forced to call, "Cut!"

which costs energy, time, and money for the reset. This is what happens in life. Do you ever feel like you just keep going around in circles? As the star of our unique stories, we all have marks we need to hit. When life calls "Action," many times we decide to go the other way or perhaps not move at all. Success has a plan for you to live a fulfilled existence and when we don't hit our marks, it causes confusion and derails us. Life keeps happening and playing forward; the cameras keep rolling. You can begin today to take hold of your purpose and believe in your own story by hitting your marks.

Principle #3 Sell it

In order to sell a movie, three components must be in place: packaging, marketing, and distribution. Before we can sell anything, we must first understand *what* we're selling and *whom* we are selling to. You are the marketing and distribution executive of your movie. A movie is only as good as its poster, its marketing, and its distribution. Your poster is your calling card, essence, or brand. Your marketing is the bridge that connects your consumer to your product or service and the distribution is the source of delivery. You are the only one capable of bringing your movie (passion, purpose, and gifts) to the marketplace. Sure, you can have agents, managers, and public relation firms, but it all starts with you.

Packaging: Consumers judge a book by its cover

I teach filmmakers that they don't really make movies—they make movie posters. By this I mean that their film is only as good as the poster—isn't that what an audience views first before deciding to see the film? Since you are "the movie," your packaging must be in line with what you are selling and whom you are selling to. Does your brand match your product? Does your packaging appeal to your audience?

Marketing: The profit is in the popcorn

Through many years of marketing films, I came to understand that theatre owners generally make very little money on the ticket sales of the movie; they make a fortune, however, selling popcorn. Talk about a huge markup, and even though many moviegoers complain, they still buy the popcorn. Why? They buy it because hot popcorn is part of the movie-going experience. A movie just isn't the same without a big bag of buttered popcorn. So, how does this apply to a life of success? You are offering more than you or your abilities; you are offering the experience. Many times, your profit will not directly come from the product you are selling; it will come from your byproduct. My friend and co-producer Ronny Hadar launched the successful television series *Power Rangers*. Ronny shared with me the secret to the multi-millions earned from the series: most of the money is made selling the merchandise such as Power Ranger figures, clothing, and accessories. For example, maybe you're a life coach, but your big money might be made from the new radio or television show offered to you, or your book that hits the *New York Times* bestseller list. This is the franchise concept; you are never *just* selling you or your product—you are selling your franchise, an experience. Now let's talk about *how* to get yourself and your product or talents in front of your audience.

Distribution

This day in age, compared to any other time, distribution options are limitless. With the advent of the Internet, your audience is global. However, there is one key element that most people never discover. When I first started making films, I was compensated for acting, writing, producing, and directing. However, my big payday didn't come until I retained a portion of the distribution rights. This opened up a whole new world to me and allowed me to understand the phrase *multiple streams of income*, or what I call *back-door income*, which becomes the secret to financial fortune. So keep yourself open to this new adventure called living your story and make the best of your opportunities when navigating the world of distribution.

Now that you are packaged, marketed, and distributed, it's *show time*. Will you win an Academy Award and be a box office smash? Or will you not even get the movie of your life released? This isn't referring to fame and fortune. You win at life when you fulfill your potential. Truth and quality are hallmarks of a memorable story. Live your life with purpose. Choose life, offering your gifts to others. Your Executive Producer releases only quality films. He has cast you—and only you—to play the amazing character written just for you. The red carpet has been rolled out and your fans are waiting to watch a masterpiece. But it's up to you. Your film set is built, the lights are on, and the cameras are rolling. As a director, I am officially calling, "Action!" Are you ready for your close-up?

David is available for one-on-one mentoring and speaking and consulting with groups.

He can be reached via email at David@DavidHeavener.com.

***

Contact info:

Tel. (818) 679-4642 or Skype: DavidHeavener

www.DavidHeavener.com

David@DavidHeavener.com

www.ChainedInnocence.com

https://www.facebook.com/davidheavener

https://twitter.com/davidheavener

https://www.instagram.com/davidheavener/

Cliff Waterbury

Cliff Waterbury is an inventor and researcher, currently in the process of creating a New Earth technology that has been channeled through him, over the past 15 years. As an open channel for new thought and technology, he is able to receive and interpret complex scientific data and information.

Cliff's natural ability as a channeled and empathic healer were born out of a spiritual awakening experience that enables him to see the world through new eyes.

Born and currently residing in Kingston Ontario, Cliff is in the process of authoring and collaborating on a series of inspired action books based around a character named Yabbit the rabbit. Yabbit represents several aspects of the author's life purpose and is envisioned to serve many expressions revolving around the invention.

He is also the creator of IVELOUTION which is wordplay on the phrase "I have a solution"; and serves as a collaborative research and development website for the technology.

As a recent graduate of the Inaugural Delegate Level 1 online course, offered through the Resonance Academy, he is inspired to create a lasting legacy that will serve humanity for generations to come while actively pursuing a degree in unified physics.

Walking Between Two Worlds

By Cliff Waterbury

This chapter reflects upon the introspective journey of the author. It offers a glimpse into the world of self-mastery as it pertains to the level of commitment and dedication that I have come to realize is necessary, as I venture forth into the uncertain world of inventing and co-creating with spirit. It provides a brief introduction to an exciting new technology that has been channeled through me and is currently incubating through various stages of research and development. And, it highlights some of the magical aha moments and synchronicities that have shaped my journey to this point, ultimately leading to the writing of this chapter.

I would also like to introduce you to a very unique character that I call Yabbit the Rabbit. Yabbit represents one of the main characters in the story of this inventor, and serves as a narrator to highlight the journey and outer expression of the technology that is being brought to life. He illustrates the various incarnations, or parts of my persona, that have undergone major transformation during my own journey to self-mastery. He plays an archetypal role in molding and shaping me for my life's purpose.

Part of the inspiration for Yabbit is based on how many times I have caught myself procrastinating and making excuses for not moving forward in life. In essence, procrastination and all of its derivative forms, as well as my own negative self-talk, have created a steady flow of opposition to my own progress and success. Over the years, I have learned to recognize and re-pattern my beliefs, to support the changes I have been making in my life.

Yabbit the rabbit had a bad habit. It was called procrastination.

Yabbit is also a fictional character that represents the little voice in our heads that pops in from time to time and offers us "unsolicited advice." It likes to plant a seed of doubt or cast a shadow upon our dreams and our intentions. This little voice will often appear when we are contemplating a change, or trying to better our lives in some way. No one really likes unsolicited advice. We often don't listen or take the advice anyway, especially if it is intended to criticize us in some way. So, naturally, I wonder why so many of us listen to and allow this inner voice to hold so much power over us?

How often do we doubt ourselves, or limit our experiences and our opportunities, because we are choosing to listen to this so-called voice of reason? Or perhaps it is the voice of treason, and we stop ourselves completely before attempting to do something different. We make excuses to rationalize and come up with all kinds of reasons why we can't or we won't.

How many times a day do you say to yourself or someone else, "I really wish I could do that. Yeah, but I can't." or "I would really like to try that. Yeah, but I won't because of (fill in the blank)." We all do it. Are we conscious of our own self-talk or are we so programmed and conditioned to run on autopilot that we don't even notice and realize we're saying it? You might be surprised when you realize just how often it shows up in our lives. Our negative self-talk and deeper core beliefs are constantly running in the background of our lives and they hold us in place, often sabotaging our success. Perhaps, now that I have brought it to your conscious attention, you may notice that little voice that pops in from time to time and says, "Remember me?"

It takes consistent effort and practice, but the more we become consciously aware of them and the effects they are having on our lives, the better we are able to help ourselves get past the blocks to our own success. Becoming aware and more present in our lives is like seeing the world through new eyes.

We are all on a journey.

We are all on a path that is leading us home, back to ourselves and in the direction of our hearts. We are in the process of reclaiming who we really are and finding our deeper purpose for being. We are continually being guided and inspired to seek our own answers and to open our hearts and unlock the wisdom and truth that lies within.

My journey began to unfold in October of 2002, with a spiritual awakening experience that planted the seeds for the new technology and the envisioned book series, Yabbit the rabbit.

It was an instantaneous awakening and transformational experience that expanded my conscious awareness to a whole new level of being and understanding. It opened my heart and deepened my connection to my higher self. It shifted my concept and perception of reality, and introduced me to an often unseen and magical world that exists all around and within us. In essence, I began seeing the world through new eyes and from the perspective of the heart. I was awakened to a greater truth and shown my real purpose for being here. The experience was an initiation and activated my soul's higher calling and has, ultimately, shifted my life into a new reality. I have been tapped into the quantum field or universal mind ever since.

While the experience shifted my concept and perception of reality in that moment, it has been a step-by-step healing and transformational process to bring my mind into alignment with my heart. A large part of my journey has been to understand, accept, and integrate the knowledge and the wisdom that has been shifting my consciousness, from the inside out, ever since. I have been led through a very conscious and deep exploration of my own heart and mind. Throughout the process of transformation, I have overcome many of my own limiting beliefs and self-sabotaging behaviors and patterns. It has certainly been a challenge to differentiate between the two very different perspectives and viewpoints of reality and find the delicate balance between them. My journey into self-mastery has taught me how to be more self-aware and present, while developing a very unique skill set that allows me to act as a bridge or channel between two worlds. I am able to tap into the universal mind, or connect with my higher self, and bring forth new information that is relevant to the new thought and scientific realms.

It was shortly after my awakening that I began receiving guidance and inspiration for a new technology. I was downloaded with a blueprint or template of scientific information and what was to be the beginning of an instruction manual for a new energy device. That was 15 years ago, and was my first introduction to channeling and the concept of automatic writing. It also marked the beginning of my own personal journey into the world of self-mastery. It launched me into the world of quantum physics, igniting my curiosity and inspiring my own scientific exploration into the concept of a unified field theory. The majority of my research revolves around the new physics model and aligns with the information that I continue to receive.

There have been many unexplained and bizarre coincidences over the past 15 years of my life that defy human logic and challenge the intellectual mind. They would have to be experienced, or witnessed, to appreciate and capture the essence of how significantly they have influenced my journey. My life has certainly been an interesting adventure and continues to unfold through a string of synchronicities and magical moments. Many of these have shifted my own conscious perception and led me to the next step or piece of the puzzle. In essence, they have become the roadmap to my success. They always seem to be pushing the boundaries of my resistance to change and encouraging me to step out of my comfort zone. The more I allow the process to unfold and get out of my own way, the more coincidences and opportunities tend to magically appear, including the opportunity to write this chapter and become a published author.

I chose the name IVELOUTION for my website because it represents the scope of my research and the various embodiments of the technology. It is wordplay on the phrase "I have a solution" and was a word that popped into my mind during a meditation. In this meditation, I was led through a visualization exercise that showed me the conceptual design of the device and the actual process that would unfold within the combustion chamber of the surrounding unit.

This particular visualization stands out in my mind as a major turning point or milestone in my life. It was the first time that I truly believed and trusted in the information I had been receiving. Up until that point, I had been downloading all kinds of scientific data and drawings, but none of it seemed related or connected to a specific device.

Several years earlier, I had a recurring dream where I was seeing different aspects or components of the system, but it was not as defined as it was in this visualization. I would try to capture as many of the images in my mind's eye as I could, but was not able to hold the space long enough or remember the details. This often occurred when I first opened up to receiving messages. I would get excited and just start writing or drawing, often in the middle of the night, and forgot what I was seeing or couldn't get the information written down fast enough. Part of the process of transformation has been learning to hold my attention and focus for long periods of time.

This was often frustrating and nerve-racking for me, but with continued practice, I eventually learned to shut the mind out and allow the information to flow through me, rather than trying to direct and figure it out in my head.

Seeing the device in my mind's eye was a major aha moment, and I remember feeling a calm and renewed sense of purpose come over me. It was an intuitive knowing that this was what I was meant to do. Having this particular realization led me to seek further scientific consultation, while continuing my own independent research. It was also a catalyst for other key events and milestones that have been miraculously occurring ever since my awakening.

I began diving into periodicals on quantum physics and searching the Internet, but found very little information to substantiate or validate the information I was receiving. At the time, I was able to type several words into the Google search engine and get no results. My intuition was telling me that I was definitely on to something, even though I wasn't yet sure what I had.

Through another series of coincidences, I was guided to the Resonance Project and the ground-breaking research of Physicist Nassim Haramein and his unified field theory. In 2012, I attended one of his delegate workshops to explore his work and learn more about unified physics. I remember being blown away by the depth and clarity with which he was able to explain the material, and by the science that was uniquely similar to the information I had been receiving over the past several years. I became a participant and graduate of his inaugural, online Delegate Level 1 course, which was a much more interactive and experiential immersion in his life's work and the new unified physics.

This gave me further confirmation, and through his ongoing research and teachings, I have been able to strengthen my own understanding and comprehension of the physics and scientific information I continue to receive.

To date, I have received several thousand pages of drawings, schematics, and scientific information for a new energy technology, along with many new processes that filter into several new emerging fields of scientific research. The majority of my own research, and the information that I continue to receive, offer sustainable and relevant solutions to many of the world's current and pressing ecological challenges. These technologies and processes will help to bridge the gap between science and spirituality, as well as restore the earth back to her natural state.

As an ongoing contributing member and sponsor of the Resonance Academy, I have attended many of the online forums and breakout sessions and have maintained a dialogue with several of my fellow graduating delegates from the course. It is through the reach of the Academy that I have been able to connect with so many passionate souls who share a similar vision and unique skill set to complement my own. Together, we are collaborating to create a more sustainable future for generations to come.

Part of being on the path to self-mastery, and becoming more aware and present in my life, has been developing better trust, faith, and belief in the things I cannot see, but somehow know.

Having faith and trusting your intuition, as well as listening to your inner guidance, is certainly challenging and often goes against the mind's wishes of playing it safe or waiting to figure it out in your head. One of the challenges for me has been in allowing the process of my journey to unfold, rather than trying to figure out the next step. I have found that as I dive deeper into the process, I can accomplish a lot more in a short period of time with the right mindset, as opposed to being scattered and going in several directions at once.

We are so programmed to do and focus on achieving results that we often don't allow for synchronicity or life's little nuances to unfold and lead us to the next step. I have learned through experience to get out of my own way and allow things to progress naturally, rather than pushing to accomplish or do something. If something isn't lining up or coming together as I had expected, or I'm finding it difficult to connect with someone or move forward easily, then there is usually a reason and it could be that the timing isn't quite right.

Learning to balance divine timing and follow my intuition has not been easy at the best of times. This is especially true when it comes to knowing about the technology and the exciting possibilities and opportunities it will create, not to mention the positive impact it can have on the world. Learning to be patient and maintaining a day-to-day routine and paying the bills, instead of just going for it, has proved to be quite difficult for me. I did try to just go for it a couple of times, but quickly realized I needed a better plan and financial base in order to remain focused and in the right mindset. Having this base would enable me to receive guidance, while preventing my deeper fears from surfacing and sabotaging my success.

The daily routine has provided the foundation and allows me to stay grounded as I continue to pursue my dream and navigate the technology forward. Learning to stay in the moment allows me to focus on the larger picture, while concentrating on the details that are necessary for my future aspirations. It also keeps me from getting caught up in the events unfolding on the world stage.

The more I shift my attention away from the collective mindset and the ongoing stream of distractions, and concentrate on my inner world, the better able I am to focus and be of service to others. By shifting my own focus and concentrating on my inner world, I have found that more coincidences occur, more possibilities open up, and I create opportunities that I would have otherwise missed if my focus had been elsewhere, such as on a world event. It is amazing to realize how a simple shift in our own conscious perception, or looking at things from a different viewpoint, can often lead to amazing breakthroughs or realizations.

Trusting my guidance, having faith in the unknown, and believing in what I could not consciously see has proved to be very rewarding for me.

The wisdom of the heart knows what the mind is constantly seeking. Learning to accept divine timing rather than forcing things to fit into the constructs of my own expectations has taught me compassion, patience, and to appreciate what is right in front of me. Offering hope, or a kind word of encouragement to others, is what inspires me to continue along my path and into the next chapter of my life.

Writing this chapter and sharing part of my journey with an audience has been an emotional clearing and healing process in its own right, but has also allowed me to step beyond my boundaries and comfort zone to take a leap of faith into the unknown. Even though the process has revealed another layer of my own resistance to change, I knew I had to take the risk in order to evolve and advance the technology to the next level. I have come to realize that the more I get out of my own way and step beyond my limitations, the more magical the journey becomes.

Part of my life's journey has been learning to walk between two worlds and maintain a foothold in each. Wherever your journey takes you in life, know you are loved and being gently guided in the directions of your dreams.

To learn more about the ongoing progression of the project, its origins, and the science and technology, please visit www.Iveloution.com, or hop on over to YabbittheRabbit.com, for a more in-depth look at the author and the revolving story around the technology.

***

To contact Cliff:

www.Yabbittherabbit.com

www.Iveloution.com

linkedin/CliffWaterbury

facebook/CliffWaterbury

Jennifer Beilsmith

Jennifer Beilsmith, M.S.Ed, is a certified life coach, speaker, and author who works with clients from all over the world. Jenny believes that "we all hold the power within us to change." Through the coaching process, Jenny supports her clients to connect to their inner power. She helps them to get aligned with their true desires, create plans, take consistent action, reach their goals, and become their best self. Jenny's authentic and engaging personality makes her easy to relate to. She founded The Prosperous Path, where she coaches clients in one-on-one sessions and leads dynamic workshops and seminars. Her expertise has been featured in many newspapers and magazines. Jenny can relate firsthand to many of life's challenges as a wife, mother of twins, and Christian professional. With a true passion for personal development, Jenny's goal is to empower her clients to stop making excuses and live authentically in both their personal and professional lives.

The Power Within

By Jennifer Beilsmith

Life is full of possibilities. I have always believed that we have the choice and the power within us to create our own life stories exactly as we want them to be. We each have unique gifts that, when expressed, allow us to live the truth of who we are. Believing in these gifts and unleashing this power can be challenging. We are so accustomed to focusing on our weaknesses and problems that often times we cannot see our greatness.

My path to seek, discover, and reveal my inner power and authenticity has been a challenge. Over the past decade, I have been on a personal journey filled with many lessons and experiences that have allowed me to uncover many truths. It has not been easy; but it's been a journey that has changed me and one that I feel compelled to share. My hope is that as you read about my journey, you will be empowered to find your own power within and become your best self.

One of the most challenging questions that I had to answer was—who is the authentic me? I often felt that part of me had been hiding for a very long time. Deep inside, I knew that the path to fulfillment and peace was through expressing this person. However, it felt uncomfortable to open up. I wondered if I could do this and, if so, how? I heard a small whisper and felt a little nudge from God, pushing me to grow. These persistent, inner nudges coerced me into pursuing an inner journey to explore my true self.

I decided that first I had to uncover the beliefs and thoughts that were holding me back from being me. I needed to find out what was untrue and out of alignment. It was hard to uncover these, because—as most of us do—I had held on to them so closely and tightly for a huge part of my life. We are programmed with these beliefs as little children. Societal rules and regulations guide our everyday actions, and we lose touch with our freedom to choose and our self-expression. We take ownership of circumstances and experiences that have happened to us. We allow others' thoughts and opinions to dictate our self-worth. We make assumptions based on our external experiences and believe them to be true. Every time we engage in one of these limiting beliefs, we distance ourselves from our real inner power, joy, and fulfillment.

After reflection, I realized that many of the beliefs that I held were untrue. I held on to lies such as "I am not good enough" and "I have to be perfect." Holding on to these caused me much doubt and fear. I had allowed them to dictate and control me for so long that it had become a habit. As I uncovered these lies, I knew I had to question and release them. I considered questions such as: "Is this thought or belief true? How does this thought or belief limit my true potential? What could unfold if I were to let go of this belief?"

I learned that each time a negative thought came up, I had to acknowledge it and recognize it as just that—a thought and not the truth. Over and over again, I reframed these thoughts and replaced them with positive statements of what's possible.

This process took time. I had to make a daily choice to change my inner dialogue. I had been letting my habits and negative thoughts dictate my self-worth. Self-awareness allowed me to change my thinking, and eventually the negative thoughts started to fade away. I experienced a new sense of freedom and peace. By removing these limiting beliefs, I was able to see my life through a new perspective of unlimited possibilities. As Norman Vincent Peale advised, "Change your thoughts and you change your world."

The Change[10]

I started to get back in touch with who I am deep inside, opening up to my true nature and following my soul's guidance. I realized I am good enough, and I am perfect just as I am. I reconnected with my little girl inside—the one who was given the nickname Sunshine because of her positive outlook and big dreams. I always wanted to make a big impact on the world, and now I once again believed I could. This journey inward was helping me get back in touch with the dynamic part of me.

Have you ever felt that way? Maybe you were a courageous and passionate child with big dreams, too. I believe that child is still inside all of us. However, we get so caught up in our busy life that we forget to take a step back and focus on what's really important.

If connecting with our real self is so important, why, then, is it so challenging? One reason could be that most of us live our days in the logical part of our minds. We are busy thinking, taking control, making judgments, doing tasks, analyzing, and solving problems. Our chattering minds have us running all over the place. We act out our deepest fears and insecurities and are not fully in touch with our emotions. Because our minds speak so loudly, directing how we spend so much of our time, we often lose touch with our inner guidance system. The challenge can be in learning to connect, trust, and respect the symbiotic relationship that is possible using our head and heart together.

As we connect to our hearts, we can experience life much differently. We become connected to our feelings, intuition, and divine wisdom. This is truly the essence of our being. We find that this intuition truly knows what is best for us. I have seen this in my own life, as well as in the lives of others. Being connected to my heart allows me to discover myself and God on a whole new level.

Connecting to these feelings and hearing this inner voice can be difficult in our busy society with so many constant distractions readily available. Some of us have buried this voice under many layers of pain, grief, doubt, and fear. Others don't know how to hear that voice. And then there are those who live in denial that they have any choice or control over their lives. Ultimately, we have to sit still and listen.

Because I love being busy, sitting in peace and quiet is a challenge for me. I have a non-stop mind that is curious and likes being engaged. A few years back, my body was trying to send me clues that what I was doing was too much. I started experiencing anxiety and felt overwhelmed. I did not want to listen and decided to carry on with business as usual. Staying busy was a tactic that I used so that I did not have to listen to or face what was really calling for attention. The truth was that I did not really want to hear what I needed to hear.

For me, searching for answers and direction from everyone else in my life seemed easier. I would call friends and ask them to listen as I ruminated about the same story over and over again. I guess I thought that if I talked about it enough, I would feel better. Sometimes it worked, but mostly I just ended up with everyone else's opinions. Finally, I realized that it did not matter how many people I shared my story with; I still felt confused and had no answers. Ultimately, it was between me and God.

Deep down, I always knew that all of my life's answers were within me. So why, then, was I ignoring this gift? The reality was that I did not know how to ask or listen for this guidance. What I found is, if we are open to it, life always blesses us with what we need.

I was guided to an amazing mentor and friend, Dr. Becky Brittain, who taught me how to be aware, check-in, and listen. I started making time daily to experience stillness through meditation, prayer, or being out in nature. I started tuning into myself.

At first, it was an uncomfortable and confusing process. My inner voice had been suppressed for so long, it was having a hard time being heard. Eventually, I started to notice a small, quiet whisper inside. Over time, it became louder and clearer. I recognized this voice as my authentic self, my soul speaking with God's guidance. This guidance came as words, ideas, or feelings of peace. I explored what these answers meant, gained clarity, and inquired what to do next. Often, I was guided to a solution or could sense what decision should be made.

This daily check-in also allowed me to reconnect with my body and sense how it was feeling. Was I relaxed and calm? Was there any tightness in my body and where? Now that I was open to listen, my heart was speaking through my body and giving me answers. This helped me gauge if I was doing too much, feeling anxious or peaceful. This process was life changing for me. It allowed me to finally hear my inner wisdom and allowed my body the ability to communicate with me. Tapping into my body's intelligence was another way I was learning to integrate all aspects of myself.

Stillness taught me another important life lesson—the power of living in the present moment. It seems that somewhere along the way, I became fixated on the past and worried about the future. I was allowing these thoughts to steal my joy on a daily basis.

I started to practice gratitude during this quiet time. Thinking grateful thoughts helped me refocus my mind on the present moment as I shifted from what was lacking in my life to the abundance that was already present. The more that I was able to do that, the fewer expectations I put on myself and the less I worried. I allowed my life to unfold more naturally.

Zen master Thich Nhat Hanh beautifully states, "If we are not fully ourselves, truly in the present moment, we miss everything."

Living in the present moment has allowed me to be aware and open to receiving God's guidance. Connecting to myself in these different ways has changed me. I guess all this time I was afraid of what my true inner voice would say to me. I now know it is the most loving presence that guides me to unleash my greatest purpose. I am not saying it is always easy, as I often resist, but then I start moving in the right direction. This connection has allowed me to realize that most of the limits in my life were self-imposed. Listening to this inner knowing has allowed me to trust myself and create my story in ways that are much bigger than anything I would have dreamed of.

The power to dream big and create what we want is inside each of us. If this is true, many might ask, then why are so many of us not living our dreams and not living in joy, but just surviving? It might have to do with the stories that we play over and over in our minds. We limit our actions with negative self-talk and bad habits. We overlook our uniqueness and special gifts. We let doubts, uncertainty, shame, and vulnerability derail us time and time again. We make it hard to feel worthy as we compare ourselves to others and our accomplishments to the world's definition of success. We do not believe in ourselves. While these feelings are a part of life, the real problem lies in letting this fear and these thoughts and feelings dictate our actions and who we are.

Author and spiritual teacher Marianne Williamson shares that "Our deepest fear is not that we are inadequate. Our deepest fear is that we are powerful beyond measure. It is our light, not our darkness that most frightens us. We ask ourselves, 'Who am I to be brilliant, gorgeous, talented, and fabulous?' Actually, who are you not to be? You are a child of God. You're playing small does not serve the

The Change[10]

world. There is nothing enlightened about shrinking so that other people won't feel insecure around you. We are all meant to shine, as children do. We were born to make manifest the glory of God that is within us. It's not just in some of us; it's in everyone. And as we let our own light shine, we unconsciously give other people permission to do the same. As we are liberated from our own fear, our presence automatically liberates others."

One of my deepest fears was of my personal power. Slowly, I opened up and realized that it was time to let my light shine. I did not have to hide my greatness anymore. I could be me. It did not matter what the world thought of me, but what I thought and felt in my heart.

It was time to authentically express myself. The problem turned out to be that I was extremely good at shaping myself to fit those around me. I was afraid to say what I really thought or felt. I justified this to myself by saying I was being nice and I didn't want to hurt or offend anyone. But I soon realized that I was hiding my opinion and doing a disservice to myself and others.

I learned how to speak the truth through conversations with a friend. She was always straight and to point—the good, the bad, or the ugly. She was able to do it in the kindest ways, and it never felt harsh or rude. I started to value this, and I knew I could count on her honesty. I began to wonder who in my life needs to hear the truth from me. Deciding to honestly express myself without fear of any consequence took courage. I was finally able to say yes when I meant yes and no when I meant no. Finding this voice has given me the freedom to speak with integrity.

It was not easy, and I am sure there are some I have offended with this way of communication. My words might have made others feel uncomfortable or many might have judged me. I came to accept this and continued to stand in my power.

I started to think about what was possible for me. What could I achieve if I fully opened up to this power within? I realized that I had been playing small and putting up walls to keep me safe. My soul, however, felt contained as I continually chose to stay in a safe space. The pain of staying still and being inauthentic became worse than the fear of being vulnerable or the fear of the unknown. Ultimately, I had to reprogram how I saw myself.

Changing my thinking was a challenge. I had to make a daily choice to redirect my negative or fearful mindset. To get different results, I had to change my beliefs. I made vision boards to link my thoughts and emotions to what I desired. I stated positive affirmations over and over again to create new pathways in my mind. I prayed, asking for courage, perseverance, and strength. I created powerful intentions to manifest what I desired. I grew in conviction in the belief that anything is possible. I always knew this was the truth, but my previous lack of self-belief had stalled my actions many times. Believing in myself was a key piece to attracting and creating more in my life.

I believe that we are all meant for more. Our lives are not about just existing, but are about evolving. Growth and change are an important part of life. But, it's not always easy. Resistance will show up. It might get uncomfortable and feel overwhelming. We can decide to work through it, or we can decide to stay stuck and stand still. All of our struggles can make us stronger and teach us if we allow them to. We have the ability to rise above them and reveal our greatness through these trials. Until we take ownership of our actions, feelings, thoughts, and mindset, we cannot change. It is a choice. The beauty of our lives is that we have the power to create and choose our thoughts and actions in every moment.

As I walked this journey, I embraced many new beliefs, uncovered and connected to the real me, found my inner voice, and listened to my body's wisdom. Stepping into my power has allowed me to be confident, speak my truth, grow in faith, take risks outside of my comfort zone, and create meaningful relationships. This journey has changed my life in ways I had not imagined. All of this was really about connecting to myself in a new way. It was not about holding myself to some impossible expectations. My days are still filled with challenges, but I now see things from new perspectives.

Author Steve Maraboli states, "You were put on this earth to achieve your greatest self, to live out your purpose, and to do it courageously."

My wish is that you will be inspired to connect to your power within, step into your greatness, and manifest all that you want for your life.

You can do it. Be yourself. Show others the real, imperfect, and beautiful person that you are. Listen to your heart. Express the greatness that is already within you. Create an extraordinary life. Be courageous. Take inspired action. Anything is possible.

***

To contact Jennifer:

jenny@theprosperouspath.com

www.theprosperouspath.com

Josephine Harewood

Josephine's aim is to help as many persons as possible to live a better life. To do this, she utilizes her experiences and skills to help supervisors, managers, high-stressed professionals, and small- and medium-sized companies find solutions to both their personal and business challenges. She is of the view that at times we all need to wake up and take some kind of positive action to propel us forward on our life journey.

Her background includes: Operations Management, Policy Development, Human Resource Management, Health and Nutrition, Life Coaching, and Social Media Marketing.

She is featured as a co-author with some leading business and motivational industry experts and best-selling authors like Brian Tracy, Denis Waitley, and Tom Hopkins in the book *101 Great Ways to Compete in Today's Job Market*.

She is also very involved in volunteer work by mentoring young people, visiting, consoling, and praying for the sick, especially cancer patients and the elderly.

Wake up! Wake up!

By Josephine Harewood

This is dedicated to the person who needs to wake up and live a better life. If you are searching for your true purpose, going through pain at home or on the job and do not know what to do, I pray that something in this article will empower you to live a better life.

The truth is that nobody wants to know about you just for knowing's sake, so wake up. We all use Knowledge to empower ourselves. We need a sense of satisfaction. According to Maslow, we all want to feel appreciated and loved. We want more money, a new house, a good job, and the love of our lives. We are all looking for our true purpose. We are so focused on our wants that we fail to see why we exist. Then we say life is not fair. Hubert Koh once said it is not fairness you want, but opportunities so "Do not ask for fairness in your life but instead ask for opportunities."

Wake up—It is about time you recognize who you are and that you are here for a purpose, and you can use this knowledge to empower and guide you through your life's journey.

Who are you?

Have you ever been to a place and the person asks "Who are you?" Knowing who you are can provide some insight into how you answer this question. Marc, a tall tanned full-bodied Sales Representative, in response to such a question would normally stand up straight, chest protruding out, and in a heavy well-pronounced masculine tone say "Marc Martis." Everyone in the room certainly looks up and now knows his name, but who really is Marc Martis? Do they know he is a workaholic juggling two jobs, can be very aggressive, and has a sense of self-awareness about his masculine competence? So who are you? Are you aware that you have been given access to all the gifts and skills you need to survive? Do you know that you have the power to do and be whatever you want to do and be? The question is, do you really want to know who you are, and are you prepared to change to be that person?

Your true potential

You said yesterday that you would do something to achieve your dreams tomorrow. It is today, and you have not yet taken action, because you are afraid that you do not know your true potential. Let me ask you: If you had all the money you wanted, and you knew you couldn't fail, what would you do? What would you change? Are you still waiting for the right time? Or are you still listening to the naysayers:

– it is not the right time for you;

- that's the stupidest idea I have ever heard;

- you are too young or you are too old;

- you do not have what it takes to do this.

According to Gary V., Wine Library TV & Vayner Media Founder, "There has never been a better time, in the history of time, than right now to start a business." So what are you waiting for? Are you still building someone else's dream? What about yours? At the end of the twenty or thirty years in your job, you are going to wake up and realize that you have nothing to show for it, since it cannot sustain you until that time arrives when you are called by the Creator.

We all have gifts, but sometimes we do not recognize these gifts.

The Change[10]

The paralyzed man in the Bible was told to take up his things and walk. We all can walk. It is a God-given gift; he had that gift. Jesus Christ said if you want to walk, take up your things and walk. You need to take action on those dreams and goals that you have hidden inside. Who told you that you have no potential? How do they know? You are the only one who knows what you can and cannot do. Are you allowing people to control what you should do or what your life should be? You may be in a good job now, with great pay and benefits, and you are doing well, but if this is not your true purpose, your enthusiasm will soon begin to fade. Discovering your true potential and true purpose can be very costly.

So how do you discover your true potential? Potential by definition is your God-given gifts and talents. Some people have the gift of creativity, others the softer skills such as caring and patience, like doctors, nurses, and to an extent teachers. You can also acquire some skills as you go along because of the experience you gain. This experience is wisdom. This is what can keep you steering in the right path and assist you to be humble, make the right decisions, and associate with the right people. True potential is what you are good at and sometimes takes time to discover. As SPANX Founder Sara Blakely says, "Embrace what you don't know, especially in the beginning, because what you don't know can become your greatest asset."

What is your vision? You see, we all need a vision. Something to empower and move us forward. There is no benefit in acquiring the unique lifestyle of Solomon Grundy as highlighted in the English Nursery Rhyme:

'Solomon Grundy- Born on a Monday.

Christened on Tuesday - Married on Wednesday.

Took ill on Thursday - Grew worse on Friday.

Died on Saturday - Buried on Sunday.

And that was the end of Solomon Grundy.'

There is more to life than this. God has a vision for you. He wants you to be great and He wants good things for you, so why shouldn't you have a vision for yourself?

Your purpose is what you want to accomplish and why. Without a strong "why," you cannot accomplish your purpose. Why do you want to lose weight? Why do you want more money? Why do you want to live a better life? To achieve our why, we must empower ourselves by having control over what we do.

Dealing with your emotions

Why are you letting people control your emotions? So you stop the car to let someone pass and the person never waved or acknowledged your kind gesture. Consequently, you allow yourself to become annoyed. Why should you become annoyed with them? There were no conditions in the first place on the gesture. It is up to the person to acknowledge your gesture. Sometimes we impose expectations on people, not realizing that we never shared those expectations with them. So how would they know how to respond? We then get annoyed; we inevitably become swept up in our emotions, causing our stress level and blood pressure to escalate. For what? That other person is going about their life and may not even give a second thought about your kind gesture.

Wake up! Wake up! You are giving people power over you without even knowing it.

A year ago, my husband and I were shopping for a new car. When we entered the car showroom, the scent of cigarettes from the Sales

The Change[10]

Representative who greeted us was so overwhelming that it was agonizingly difficult for my husband to discuss his intended purchase with that Representative. In discussing the incident some time later, I enquired why he would give anyone power over him. In explaining to him that he was allowing people to control how he feels, and as such was giving them power over him, I realized that day that I was also guilty of giving people power over me. I had to change, since I was wasting all that energy on becoming annoyed when I could have used it to empower myself. What about you? How many times have you gotten annoyed today, this week, this month? Some people get so angry they become aggressive, destroying stuff, and in relationships abusing their partners and their children. The only way to deal with this is to realize that you alone have the power to change and that you are giving up this power every time you get annoyed. Every time you lash out at somebody, you are giving away your power.

Instead of being angry with everyone and blaming everybody, maybe it is time to forgive and move on. You see, forgiving the person means you are now free, you are empowered, and no one is holding you back because of what you or they did.

Friend, you can change. You hold the key to empower yourself. According to the writer in Proverbs 29:10-18: "Fools give vent to their anger, but the wise keep themselves under control." So the next time you are angry, may I suggest you take a deep breath, count to ten, and walk away. Promise yourself that you will never give away the power that was given to you by allowing someone else to control you. You can walk away from all the chaos, because you have a choice.

There is chaos everywhere

Look around you—according to the media, there is chaos all over. The more they broadcast about chaos, the more they find opportunities for chaos. Where is your focus? Are you focused on chaos in your life, your job, or your relationship? We all know that where there is chaos, there is doubt and fear. When we doubt ourselves and are fearful that bad things will happen, then our minds start wandering. *What if this happens? What if that happens?* Wake up. Wherever you focus your energy, that is the result you will get.

According to the Bible, whatever you believe so it be done unto you. I know someone who keeps repeating "What chaos?" and everywhere he goes he encounters some chaos. What about you? Look at your life, the things you do not like or are trying to stay away from are the things that are happening in your life right now. Change your focus and re-channel your energy to the things you want. Start telling yourself: "I can't be going through this for nothing; something good will come out of it." When you look at life, out of every bad thing something good happens. But you must be open to claim and receive the good that God has for you.

I recall on one occasion my job was not very challenging and every day I would record in my diary "I have a wonderful job with wonderful pay." About six months to a year later, my husband got a contract in the Bahamas. We stayed in Paradise Island for approximately three years. I could not have asked for anything better than this experience. I could have said no and stayed where I was comfortable. To be open to your good, you have to take action. Wake up and claim the good that is yours. There is no shortage of good, just the limits you put on yourself, and no one needs to tell you this.

Why didn't someone tell me about this before?

How many times have we heard this? How are we expected to learn if we have to go through every experience first?

Are you expected to make things up as you go along? Without a plan, that is exactly what would happen—chaos, lack of focus, etc. You would never know what's happening to you. Maybe you do not know what to put in the plan, so let's go:

What are you trying to accomplish?

What is causing pain in your life?

What have you always dreamed of doing and being and felt you could not do or be?

What have you always wanted but could never afford?

Put a date on what you want to accomplish, breaking it into small action steps that you can realistically accomplish.

Once you decide on what you want to do or be, always keep your focus. Never let distractions get in your way.

Stop feeling sorry for yourself. Sorry is a recipe for attracting people who are sorry for themselves, who ultimately unleash more depression and discouragement on you. You see, God did not give you a spirit of fear and doubt. Wake up! Wake up! You are not the first one to go through crisis after crisis. You are not the first one to be abused, to lose your job, get a divorce, or to lose someone you love and you will not be the last one. Many successful people have gone through these situations and they were able to bounce back and make something out of their lives. People like Oprah Winfrey, Brendon Burchard, and Anthony Robbins all had their various issues, but they used them to bounce back, helping themselves and others. We all have the power to have a resilient ego, to be successful, enjoy life, and help others do the same.

Although it is hard to do, when you receive criticism, don't be defensive—look for the good in it. Sometimes God speaks to us in various ways and this may very well be a message for you, so be open. As the saying goes: 'God knows and God shows.'

Believe in yourself. If you do not believe that you can accomplish what you set out to do, no one else will.

Stop wanting to control other people's lives. Too often we are quick to tell other people what they should do, and we become annoyed when they do not take our advice, but our lives are in shambles and we do not want them to know what is going on with us. Deal with your issues first before you tell others how to deal with theirs.

Always be open to possibilities in achieving your dreams. If you are too closed-minded, you will miss the opportunities that are sent your way. To do this, make it a habit to pray and meditate at the start of your day. Do so for a minimum 5 to 10 minutes. Just be still and feel your oneness with God, acknowledging that He is there with you always, thanking Him and placing all your activities, needs, and dreams for that day in His hands.

Keep track of your accomplishments, regardless of how small they are, and celebrate them. Thank God that you were able to get so far.

There is no quick and easy road to success, so do the right and ethical thing to achieve your dreams. There are many get rich opportunities claiming you can do the minimum or nothing and the money will come. Always research an opportunity, even if you have a gut feeling about it. Is it in keeping with what you want to achieve and your talents/skills? Is the company stable? Is there training? What are people saying about the company?

Learn to truly appreciate people.

The spirit of love

Where is the love if we stay away from the family member or friend who we had an issue with? Wake up, wake up. We have the love inside, but we are afraid to let it go, not knowing that true love happens only when you let go and give it away. We were all given the spirit of love. While love can be very judicious, we need to see good in everyone without discriminating. True love is when you can appreciate people for who they are and what they do. Do you appreciate the people you live and work with or do you take them for granted? Are you just expecting them to do certain things and the day this does not happen, you are ready to admonish them? When was the last time you told them you appreciate them, or you appreciate what they do and truly mean it? Where is the love? Get out there and empower yourself by truly appreciating people. Smile from the heart, forgive and mean it, give without expecting anything back. Practicing empowerment through appreciation and love can be eminently inspiring.

Social needs

Have you ever noticed when an elderly person is placed in a Geriatric Home away from their family, most of them do not live very long? Scientists have discovered that spending quality time with friends and family has a positive impact on our health. This was a study conducted by a team at the University of North Carolina at Chapel Hill. Learn to enjoy the company of those persons who support and uplift you. The networking, the family gatherings, and the impromptu get-togethers all have benefits. You are not in a world by yourself; you need people to interact with, to share your ideas with, and to learn from.

You are not going to get there alone

The people who reach the top did not get there alone and the only way to stay at the top is to climb with others, side by side, instead of walking over them. Oprah Winfrey got to the top by helping others. Without her team and the viewers of her program who resonate with her experiences through *The Oprah Winfrey Show*, she would not have achieved the success she now enjoys. Bill Gates through Microsoft achieved success by helping people and companies achieve their full potential. 5Linx Diamond Senior Vice Presidents Curt and Tishina Anderson empower themselves and their teams by not only showing them the way, but also helping some of the members of their team achieve Senior Vice President status. To be empowered, you cannot tell others they are on the wrong road; you need to show them the way or take them with you. At the same time, you have to remember that there will always be a winner and a loser. The important thing is that you always do your best.

***

To Contact Josephine:

joseylifeline@gmail.com

https://www.facebook.com/JOIPF-Consulting-Services-614490215314863/

Josephine provides weekly motivational and health tips via her website: http://joseylifeline.com

Options for living a better life can be found at: http://www2.5linx.net/joseylifeline/

Kim Malama Lucien

Kim's target is to inspire the world, by inspiring the people and businesses she works with; to inspire through leadership and by invitation and example. She helps clients do business differently, creating a sustainable future-proof business while being a contribution to its employees, customers, and the local communities—in other words, to create benevolent capitalists.

With more than 15 years in business consulting experience, she continues to have a successful career incorporating her energetic and healing skills with her business knowledge in the corporate workplace. Her ability to read people, understand others, create good working relationships and effective conflict resolution substantially contribute to her success. She's a creative genius that revamps your business or your life from the inside out. She has an innate ability to tap into and recognize your natural and unique abilities and strengths and show you how to use them to your advantage. Kim works with management to create systems that are scalable, malleable, and empower everyone in the organization to ask questions and to be decision makers, which directly improves the company and the bottom line.

Benevolent Leadership
Creating Growth & Sustainability through Empowerment

By Kim Malama Lucien

Are you willing to be a leader? Willing to lead even if no one follows? Did you think that you must have people following you to be a leader? You don't need followers. Step up. Choose to be the leader of your own life. You being you, choosing you, choosing to be a benevolent leader will create change in the world. Change for you, change for your family, change for your business, change for your employees, and change for anyone you meet. Are you ready to accept that challenge?

The future of the world and the face of business is changing, fast and dynamically! 60% of the careers our children will have do not exist today. That is a staggeringly high percentage. It clearly highlights that business and our future is constantly changing and what we create today impacts tomorrow. There is also a growing trend towards self-employment, particularly as the millennials refuse to live to work and are demanding they work to live. Be the leader of your own life. Let's clear the limiting beliefs and points of view about you and business, what business is, and what it isn't.

Before I get to the specifics of 'how' to be a benevolent leader, let's take a closer look at what I mean by benevolent leader. What is a benevolent leader? Is there something that automatically pops into your mind when you hear it? I'm guessing most of you immediately think about someone doing charity work, putting others first, or giving more to someone else than themselves. What are the actual dictionary definitions of benevolence, consciousness, and leader?

-*Benevolence* is defined as being well meaning, kind, generous and/or organized to do good things for other people.

-*Consciousness* is defined as the state or quality of awareness, or, of being aware of an external object or something within oneself. It has been defined as: sentience, awareness, subjectivity, the ability to experience or to feel, wakefulness, having a sense of selfhood, and the executive control system of the mind.

-*Leader* is defined as a person who leads as a guide or conductor; a person who directs.

Surprisingly, looking at the definitions of the components of a benevolent leader doesn't really shed very much light on what it is. It has aspects of all of the things included in the definitions, but there is much more than that to it. So what is a benevolent leader?

A benevolent leader is someone who is willing to be aware of everything. They are willing to lead no matter who follows. A benevolent leader is conscious and not only willing to know what they know, but willing to act on it. They are willing to make choices and change course moment to moment if that is what is required. They consider not just what would be the greatest contribution to others, themselves, or the planet; they consider all of it equally. They are willing to be aware of what would be the greatest contribution to everyone and everything including them; everyone is included and no one is excluded.

When I talk about being a benevolent leader, most people don't think it's important, or doesn't matter to them, either because they've decided they can't be a leader, or that leading is for business owners and CEOs. What if it isn't just for people in business? What if you can be a benevolent leader to yourself or to your husband, wife, kids, mother, father, sister, brother, etc.? Can you just take a moment and imagine what it would be like? How would your everyday life be different? What would it look like if you were being the benevolent leader of your life? Can you see perceive the amount of joy, happiness, and ease all aspects of your life would have?

Before we go any further, would you be willing to destroy and uncreate your points of view about a few things? The willingness to do this will make it easier to allow the possibilities of being a benevolent leader to show up for you. When we destroy and uncreate our point of view about something, we are not destroying and uncreating the actual thing, but rather we are destroying and uncreating all of the limitations, decisions, judgments, conclusions, computations, projections, expectations, separations, and judgments we have holding the limitation in place making it impossible to change. For example, if I ask, "Would you destroy and uncreate your relationship with your family?", you are not destroying the family or the relationships, just the limitations in those relationships currently functioning unseen in the background. Who wants to keep limitations locked in place? Would you be willing to destroy and uncreate your points of view of yourself? Your business? Your family? Your relationships? What it means to be conscious? To be benevolent? To be a leader? Are you ready and willing to allow something different to show up? To allow yourself to become aware of possibilities you've never ever considered before?

I've spent well over a decade consulting for companies, many successful and many with tons of serious issues. With time and experience, I began to see a lot of similarities that were either creating success or creating limitations for them. I've noticed a growing trend to a 'me, me, me' attitude from the top to the bottom and the bottom to the top of the organizations, a lack of accountability, an unwillingness to make a decision for fear of failure or losing their job, or everyone focused on grabbing for their little piece of the pie. I've also been able to see how this shift in focus has significantly contributed to the challenging business environment so many businesses find themselves in today. They struggle to remain a relevant and innovative player in the marketplace. They have disgruntled, overworked, underpaid, and generally unhappy employees that hate their jobs, but they need that job because they have a family to support and bills to pay. So everyone is unhappy and unsatisfied and just trudging through it. No one is performing at their best. Take a minute and look at this. You've got an entire organization full of people that aren't happy with their job, which contributes significantly to them not being happy with their life. What do you think that is going to create? Did you think it was going to create a generative, innovative, dynamic, and sustainable business? How can a bunch of miserable people create something generative, innovative, and sustainable? They can't. The current state of corporate business is showing the strains of that more and more. Previously successful businesses are failing. Sick leave and work-related stress and illness continues to rise. Everyone is overtired and overworked. It has reached a place where things must change! The current climate is not sustainable.

I was one of those people. I wasn't enjoying my work anymore. I wasn't sure I was creating anything valuable or that anything I did mattered. I was usually there to fix things, to tell people what they were doing wrong and how it needed to change. As a consultant, when people saw me coming, they immediately thought that they were in trouble and I was there to get them fired or create more meaningless work for them. It just wasn't fun for anyone.

Then one day, I had a moment where I said to myself, "I can't keep going on like this. I've got to change how and what I am doing." I started looking at what I had done, looking at what was going on at the various clients and I started identifying patterns of what worked and what didn't. Then I started asking questions about how I could be different with my life and what I could do differently to make it work better for me. And most importantly, I started asking how can who I be when I work with people create a better, more satisfying situation for the people I consult with? As it turns out, this was the key. Asking not only how can I make this better for myself, but make it better for everyone I interact with changed everything. These were my first steps into being a benevolent leader. My willingness to look at what would create more for me AND what would create more for others opened the door to possibilities that weren't there before. Suddenly, I was the consultant that everyone was happy to see show up. They knew that I would do everything I could to make things as easy as possible for them and even if that meant more work in the end, they were satisfied that the end result was the best available option and they were happy to do it as a result. They felt heard and like they were a valuable contribution to the organization. I realized that this approach empowered everyone involved to choose what worked and it was the empowerment that made a significant difference in their satisfaction, which led to improved job performance, which eventually trickled down to an improved bottom line. I've seen and experienced the benefits of this shift in focus firsthand. I believe it is the primary reason I've had such a successful consulting career to date.

We spend the majority of our adult life at work. Many of us spend more time with our 'work family' than our 'blood family,' so once I was happier at work, I took the time to see how the changes I made applied to people and life more generally. What I found was that if I applied the same concepts of considering equally what would contribute to me with what would contribute to others and applied it to my entire life, my life became better as well. These were the early seeds of me realizing I could be the leader of my own life and that my willingness to be the leader of my life was what was going to create a greater future for me and everyone else, even people I didn't personally know. It's simple really—if you're happy and in a good mood, you spread that happy energy to everyone you come in contact with. So when you talk to the grocery clerk, you are genuinely interested in them, and the energy of the conversation is positive rather than negative. Your positive energy contributes to the grocery clerk so the interactions the grocery clerk has with each customer after you is more positive, spreading another seed of positive energy, and so on and so on, and that is how the seeds of being a benevolent leader of your life spread out into the world. Can you see how easy it can be to create more and how creating more for yourself and others creates more growth and sustainability?

Does this sound interesting to you? Does it seem vital to creating a future that we all would like to be around for? I hope you said yes! And now you're probably wondering how in the world do I put being a benevolent leader into action? Here are a few tools to get you going on the path of being the benevolent leader of your life. Apply the tools to your life, to your family, and to your business if you have one.

Use the tools every day, or as often as you remember. It takes practice and the more you do it the easier and more second nature it becomes. The most exciting thing for me in using the tools is I know they create change and spread consciousness and benevolent leadership into the world like little seeds flying around everywhere and create a beautiful invitation to others to join in the fun.

<u>Ask yourself these questions every day</u> and allow the energy to speak to you and see what shows up. Follow the awareness you have and take action on it.

Who or What do I have to be and do to be the conscious, benevolent leader I'm unwilling to be right now?

What one action can I take today that will make me a benevolent leader right away?

Who or What am I resisting that if I didn't resist would allow my capacity to be a benevolent leader to actualize instantaneously?

<u>Get really clear on what YOU desire.</u> Ask—What would I like my life and living to be like? What would you like it to include? To exclude? Know what you desire to be now and in the future. I can't say enough, get clear as to what your "must have's" and "cannot live with out's" are.

As a leader, you need to know where you are going. It's a lot easier to generate, create, and actualize what you desire when you have a target to aim for. This does not mean that this is a firm, unmovable goal or target. A benevolent leader gets clear on their desires and targets by being in a constant state of question and awareness—not answers and conclusions; the journey and willingness to be more conscious today than yesterday and to live in the question is far more valuable than having an 'answer.'

<u>Ditch your Fixed Points of View!</u> A conscious, benevolent leader is always following the energy, using their awareness to ask questions and make choices. They make choices rather than decisions, judgments, conclusions, and computations. They don't function from projections, expectations, separations, rejections, and judgments. There isn't a fixed point of view that a course of action will 'succeed.' Funny enough, the letting go of all expectations creates the space for more awareness and something greater than our minds can define to show up. This is true even when the 'result' is not what you expected or isn't something you'd choose again. Benevolent leaders are always asking questions as they get more information and awareness and are willing to change directions on a dime.

Empower the people around you. This does not mean micromanaging. Lots of people think being a leader means you have to control every little detail. In fact, a large percentage of the time, the opposite is true. The more you try to control, the more you have to narrow your attention to be able to control, which continually reduces the scope of your awareness and everyone else's choice.

You empower others by allowing them to choose. By allowing them to use their awareness and to choose for themselves, sometimes they will not choose what you would choose. Allowing them to choose and receive the awareness from those choices is one of the most empowering things you can do for someone. Yes, this means it looks like it might be a mistake. What if there is no such thing as a mistake? What if every choice made is a possibility for greater awareness? Total awareness is the path to awareness of total possibility. How would your life or your business be different if you were aware of the entire menu of possibilities instead of only 1%?

Function from Question, Choice, Possibility, and Contribution. Start asking questions about choices, possibilities, and contribution. This will get you to look at things from a different point of view and will provide an enormous amount of information and clarity. Asking questions like: What question can I be? What choices do I have here? What will those choices create? What else is possible here? Who can contribute to this? What is possible we haven't already considered? Demand that your family and your employees function from question, choice, possibility, and contribution. The more people functioning from this space of awareness, the more that can be created.

When it comes to your business, re-examine profit. Take a look at what you already judge as being profitable. Have you decided that doing the same thing over and over will bring in more and more money in the future? What would you like to change? Keep the same? What future would you like to create? True profitability comes from not only the willingness to see a wide range of possibilities, but the ability to choose and institute them. Not everything will turn out well, or like you expect, so the willingness to be aware and change as necessary will create true profitability.

These are just a few simple ways to start becoming a benevolent leader. There is no 'right' or 'wrong' way to do it. It will look and feel different for every single person and every single organization. Your willingness to ask questions, to be aware, to empower everyone with choice, and to keep experimenting will expose more and more possibilities to you. The more you do it, the easier it gets. All you have to do is make a commitment to yourself and get started!

***

To Contact Kim:

www.KimMalamaLucien.com

kim@kimmalamalucien.com

https://www.facebook.com/KimMalamaLucien

Visit her website today to register for her newsletter, book a session, schedule training for your organization, or contact her!

Jo Condrill

Jo Condrill knows a secret that can change your life.

At a crossroads in her life when women had more opposition than opportunities, she had neither money nor a job. What she did have was a powerful vision. She set out to learn everything she could about how to succeed in a fast-changing world. Along the way, she documented the process that brought her success time after time.

Jo had the distinction of leading a group of 3,000 members in a Washington, DC district of Toastmasters International to rank number one in the world. She also served as a non-military leader at U.S. Army Headquarters in the Pentagon. When she went on from there, she was recognized by the Army with its highest civilian award, the Decoration for Exceptional Civilian Service.

Today, Jo Condrill is considered by many to be an outstanding mentor, author, and professional speaker. Her company, GoalMinds, Incorporated, has provided services for some of the country's most respected corporations. She is co-author of the popular book *101 Ways to Improve Your Communication Skills Instantly* and author of *Take Charge of Your Life: Dare to Pursue Your Dreams*. One reader stated, "That book ultimately saved my life."

How To Reinvent Yourself In 7 Simple Steps
Move Forward in a New Way in Your Career and Your Life

By Jo Condrill

Are you unfulfilled in your job? Unhappy with the way your life is turning out? Ready to take off in an entirely new direction? There was a time when that perfectly described me. When I became single again, I was a part-time editorial assistant for *Airman Magazine*, barely able to pay my bills. It was frightening. Luckily, I had discovered Napoleon Hill's book *Think and Grow Rich* a few years earlier. I took a risk and began to take charge of my life. I wanted to become a midlevel manager, but I was only a high school graduate. Once I put my mind to work, it didn't take long before opportunities came my way. But this isn't about me; it's about you. Using the steps I've learned can help you lead a happier, more fulfilling life.

It doesn't matter what the circumstances are; if you're not happy with your life, you can learn how to make positive changes and take charge of your future.

You can learn how to:

Reinvent yourself, personally and professionally

Go from where you are now to where you want to be

Overcome obstacles and find solutions

Prepare for pitfalls

Develop an action plan with goals and timelines for achieving them

Move confidently into the future of your dreams

Whether you're just starting out, looking to move up, or want to change course completely, consider this the makeover of your life. Don't wait. Begin now.

Step 1: Set a Starting Point with a Lifeline Exercise

You are creating the person you will become by the way you envision that person, the goals you set, and the actions you take. By exercising your free will and consciously making choices, you become co-creator with the Maker of all things.

Do you want to go to graduate school or take fun courses? Do you want to get involved in social work or climb the social ladder? These are not right or wrong or even mutually exclusive decisions, but they do lead in different directions.

A lifeline exercise which is frequently used in career planning and management might be useful to "see" how your life looks, to gain insight into your worldview, to chart relationship patterns, and to consider your legacy.

The usual lifeline is a line that extends from birth to death. However, in many cultures, more subtle perhaps in the Western world, a career is discussed, predicted, and planned by family and community well before the birth of the child.

Acknowledging this reality and addressing it will help us separate a personal vision from that of our family or community. This is not always an easy or comfortable task. We see this influence in some military families with several generations of military leaders. The firstborn, particularly, senses some expectation that he or she will follow the family tradition.

Extending the lifeline to some years past our death challenges us to consider our legacy. What do we hope or plan to leave behind us?

What contribution do we wish to make to society? What are we REALLY working toward?

This exercise is sometimes used with undergraduate and graduate business students. It is a useful tool for students to learn what work life has for them and to chart their dreams and dreads about their career into the future.

Expand the scope of this exercise and consider life in general. Identify significant events of your life and write them down. Events considered positive can be written in one column and those considered difficult or traumatic in another column.

Then take time to think. Are you allowing some of the things in the negative column to hold you back? Now is a good time to deal with them and let them go. Think about the positive things. Have you thought about all the good that you have done to help other people? Have you thought about all the accolades or kudos other people have given you? Relish them and decide to take them forward with you as you plan your future.

When you consider the future, look for significant events that are likely to take place in your future. Such events might involve aging parents, graduation, promotion, birth or death of a loved one, and so on.

The lifeline exercise will give you a snapshot of where you are now. It will show some of the events that have shaped who you are, and may encourage you to let go of things that are blocking your progress. Looking to the future, you can see some things that are likely to happen. Using the lifeline exercise will help make choices easier and more productive as you begin to develop a plan for your future.

Step 2: Dream Great Dreams

Now that you have a good grasp of where you are now, imagine you could be anything you want to be, do anything you want to do, and have anything you want to have. What would you imagine? If you could design the ideal life you would be living a year from now or three to five years from now, what would it be like? How is what you want for your future different from the life you're living today?

Step away from daily activities. Take time for yourself and think about your future. It isn't easy because most of us are so busy with daily activities we hardly have any extra time. This is important, though, for your future happiness and success.

Visualize the future of your dreams. How do you look? Where you live? Imagine your surroundings. What kind of car do you drive— or will you have a driver? What are your hobbies? Think Big! It's okay to be audacious. You don't need to be realistic; we will work through that later. Let your dreams challenge you and excite you! What if they could really come true? Let yourself go.

You may dream of becoming the Chief Executive Officer of a giant corporation. Your dream may be leaving the corporate world to build a business of your own. It could be leaving the business world altogether and going to live in a small house in the woods!

Once you've got that dream in mind, you're ready to take the next step.

Step 3: Make a Decision - Exercise Your Power to Choose

Simply dreaming great dreams will not change your life. Rather, it's what you do with those dreams that is important. We need to develop belief that our dreams are achievable. In every decision we make, we exert a power to shape and control our life. Unfortunately, instead of pursuing our own empowerment, we sometimes blame our choices on things that have nothing to do with us. How many times have you heard someone say "I had no choice" or "I couldn't help it"? Was that really the case or did the person just not understand the power of his or her personal choices? Notice how you can get distracted and let outside influences take you off course. Consider how your life changes with every decision you make, no matter how small. Take responsibility for your decisions so you can shape your ultimate path.

Check out your dreams—those images you created in your right brain. Put them through the logical process of your left brain. Why is that important? Because to achieve the dream, the left hemisphere has to believe the dream is within the realm of possibility. Only then can the subconscious mind help us make the dream happen. Again, it's important to be alone and take time to think.

What obstacles are standing in the way of your dreams? Often the obstacles that come up are lack of time, money, and know-how.

The challenge then is to look for resources. This is a good time to switch back to that creative right brain and look for solutions. Could you find another way to have more time, perhaps getting up an hour earlier, or reading time management tips and acting on them? Do you have a friend who could exchange babysitting hours with you? Do you need more money? A part-time second job might help if you have the time. Could you get someone to sponsor you by paying for some of the things you will need as you start out on your new course? These things matter and could be the beginning of a great new future for you. Think of the benefits.

You may be thinking that all you need to do is refresh your memory about the Law of Attraction and, Presto! the resources will appear. That would be nice and there's no doubt that the Law of Attraction can help us in many ways. We just have to do our part to make things happen and this step is crucial to your success.

When all your analysis is done, what matters most is if your gut says, "go with it!" And a voice in your head says, "I can do it." (I get chills just writing this. Think of the possibilities!) Without that "I can do it" message, that inner confidence and drive, the numbers will mean little. As Carl Jung, Founder of Analytical Psychology, advised, "Your vision will become clear only when you look into your heart. Who looks outside, dreams. Who looks inside, awakens." Make a commitment. Your resolve is important.

Then begin to look for ideas to make a Vision Board or Goal Poster, a visual reminder of your dream. Williams Jennings Bryan, politician and orator, said, "Destiny is not a matter of chance, it is a matter of choice; it is not a thing to be waited for, it is a thing to be achieved."

Step 4: Form a Support Team

You are amazing. You have selected a dream, analyzed it, and decided to act on it. Now the next step is to share it. Begin with the most important people in your life who you believe will be supportive. For me, it was my Aunt Nora. She was never a "Naysayer. " She would ask questions and listen. You will be more inclined to see such a person's comments as helpful, rather than criticisms. At this point, you need encouragement more than help in fine-tuning your ideas. As your belief grows stronger, you will be better able to handle opposing opinions.

Who are those people who will be most affected by your decision? Who has the greatest stake in your success? They may include your spouse or partner, your children, and immediate family members. It may be an investor, coach, or mentor. This is not about abandoning your responsibilities; it's about figuring out how to make it work within your dream.

Unfortunately, many people find it difficult to accept help. They think they should be able to do everything themselves or that they'll feel obligated to someone for their assistance. Remember, "No person is an island." No one has all the answers and there are many unique ways to pay someone back. Find support early in the process and your journey will be much more fun and rewarding.

One additional way to enroll other people is to form a mastermind group. It could be a group solely focused on your plan or it could be a group focused on interests of the individual members of the group.

A mastermind group consists of people who work together in absolute harmony and trust to achieve their goals. While these people work in harmony, they may be very different from each other. The common element is that each draws on the specialized knowledge of the others, and each contributes freely to the group.

When many minds concentrate on a single point, the activity generates a power over and above the sum total of each of the individual minds. It is as though an invisible force joins the group and provides additional insight. Personally, I have used the mastermind concept with amazing results, first to advance my career and later to lead a group of volunteers to rank number one in the worldwide organization of Toastmasters International. What a thrill it was!

Step 5: Develop a Strategy - Plan and Implement

It is not necessary to know at the beginning everything that will need to be done. You have an outcome in mind. You have analyzed it, looked at obstacles and possibilities for overcoming those obstacles. You have identified possible resources.

Now develop an idea of how you can get from where you are to where you want to be. Visualize your dream. Play with it in your mind for a few days. Think of what you will have to do to make it real. When you build a house, you begin with a foundation. You would think the same is true about building your dream. Some people find it helpful to begin at the end and work backwards as Stephen Covey, famous author of *7 Habits of Highly Effective People*, advised, "Begin with the end in mind." You need a roof. Before you can put the roof on, you will need walls. The walls will need windows and doors, and so on.

Identify the critical success factors. What must be done to ensure success and preclude failure? Your plan does not need to be elaborate or time consuming. It does, however, require some thought. Make a list of everything you can think of that needs to be done, beginning at the end when you're reached your dream. That may be a short list. Then make a "top of the head" list of everything that you now know will need to be done. That list doesn't require much thinking; just go with what comes to mind. When will you need money and how much? Will you need help from someone with specialized knowledge and in what areas? Get the assistance you need. Look for things that are building blocks to other objectives. Envision yourself already in possession of your dream.

Your next task is to sort that "top of the head" list into a logical sequence.

Then implement the plan. Many of us are put off by extensive details and formulas. However, some plan must be put into writing, so that your target is fixed and you can review it from time to time. Things don't always go according to plan, yet even a poor plan enthusiastically pursued is better than action taken with no plan. I was in the planning business long enough to experience that firsthand.

I worked on the support plan for the burial of the Unknown Serviceman from the Vietnam War. We were on the scene at the U.S. Capitol Building on the day of the burial. At the last minute, the senior generals decided to walk instead of ride in the cars we had lined up to take them to Arlington Cemetery. We had to hurry and get the cars out of the way so the funeral march could begin.

When the road seems too difficult or you become too tired, a look at your clearly defined path in the action plan can boost your spirits. Adjustments can be made to the plan along the way. Don't hesitate; take the first step today.

Step 6: Keep Score - Measure Your Progress

This next step turns your action plan into goals. Keep track of your progress and decide if where you are now is where you projected you would be. Learn from your successes and failures and determine what you need to work on to achieve your goals.

The baseline is where you are now. You saw it in your lifeline. It's your line of scrimmage. With all you have built, now it's time to move forward. If something interrupts your progress, you'll need to evaluate what went wrong, make some adjustments, and start moving again.

The goal line is your desired outcome. As you focus on the long-term goal, don't forget the short-term goals. Setting and attaining small goals helps give your self-confidence a boost and keeps you motivated to continue on the path toward your long-term goals.

Step 7: Be Grateful - Acknowledge Your Successes

Show gratitude to everyone who helps you along the way. Write them a Thank You note and mail it. Take a quick snapshot with them in it and send it to them; don't just post it on social media. It will help to keep them willing to go along with you. Don't wait to see if everything turns out all right.

Kudos for others are necessary. It's also important to reward yourself. After all, you're doing this for your benefit. Commit to paper how you will reward yourself when you reach a certain goal, and follow through. For example, take that exotic vacation you've been dreaming about or buy a new car.

Focusing on these seven steps will empower you to take charge today for a better tomorrow. The thrill in this game called "life" is charting a course, facing challenges head-on, and holding someone else's hand along the way. Sometimes you win; sometimes you lose. Either way, when you focus on the big picture and refuse to let past mistakes keep you down, you create a future that is filled with possibility. So live to the fullest in the present moment and make the most of it to achieve your vision.

***

To contact Jo:

Email: info@goalminds.com

Telephone: 210-787-9073

Skype: jo.condrill

Website: http://jocondrill.com

Website: http://mastermindmanual.com

Website: http://goalminds.com

LinkedIn: http://linkedin.com/in/jocondrill

Facebook: http://facebook.com/jocondrill

Twitter: http://twitter.com/JoCondrill

Mache Torres

Recent awards: "Woman of Distinction Award" and "Gawad Amerika Award" in Education and Philanthropic category.

Married to David Ackerman, with five beautiful daughters.

Graduated from De La Salle University with a Marketing Management Degree & Master's Degree in Educational Leadership and Management. Took ultimate advanced courses in Medical Hypnotherapy- A 5th Path Hypnotherapist and a 7th Path Self-Hypnosis teacher, graduated from the Banyan Institute of Hypnosis in Orange County, California.

A businesswoman, President/ COO of Triumphus, Inc. An educator, co-owner, and a Board of Trustee of the family-owned school business St. James College System in the Philippines. A philanthropist and a civic leader, founder of TASA - Transformational Advocacy Thru Self Awareness and Charter President of the Rotary Club of Makati Business District. Founder/ CEO of Mache Torres Advocacy & Leadership Programs, Inc.

A life coach who empowers and inspires, she specializes in traumas; childhood issues; emotional instability; self-leadership/awareness; relationships/marital problems; addiction and depression.

Co-author of the *The Change*[8] - "So Near Yet So Far"; *Passionately with No Bounds!* and *You Are Brand New!*, which will be launched soon.

Explore The Deepest Essence of Your Being

By Mache Torres

Essence in general has been defined as:

The intrinsic nature or indispensable quality of something, especially something abstract, that determines its character (*Oxford Dictionary*).

The basic nature of a thing; the quality or qualities that make a thing what it is; a substance that contains in very strong form the special qualities (such as the taste and smell) of the thing from which it is taken (*Merriam-Webster Dictionary*).

What is the truest essence of one's being? What is a person truly made of? What is the quality of life that a person should have? It speaks of one's genuine composition referring to a person's holistic structure: mentally, physically, emotionally and spiritually.

The majority of the global population have just simply defined their essence based on their material possessions and financial capability. They have a limited understanding of their essence. It is only according to what they have come to be based on their personal careers and ambitions. Some self-made persons think that they have reached the peak of their life after being successful in their own businesses, fields, or expertise. But is that the real essence of one's existence?

Based on my life's personal experiences and as a practicing life coach and hypnotherapist, I have witnessed other people's personal unique journeys. Herewith is my deeper understanding on how a person's true essence in his or her existence should be lived. I have summarized my definition by creating an acronym for the word ESSENCE:

- ➢ E - mpowered Existence with a Deep Purpose
- ➢ S - elf Leadership Guided with Spirituality
- ➢ S - trength Within
- ➢ E - nvision Your Powerful Existence
- ➢ N - urture Your Inner Child
- ➢ C - ompassionate Soul
- ➢ E - mbrace Change with Extreme Gratitude

EMPOWERED EXISTENCE WITH A DEEP PURPOSE

Are you empowered? Does your existence have the power to inspire and influence others? Are you aware of your deepest purpose in life?

An empowered individual has a clear sense of self-awareness. He or she knows himself or herself very well. A person who is aware of his or her strengths and weaknesses, most importantly, someone who has the humility to accept the weaknesses and has the openness to unlearn old negative patterns and to relearn new and powerful self-development tools.

Existence without a purpose is like a fruit tree that does not bear fruit. If you have an orange tree in your own backyard, you would expect to enjoy fresh orange juice every morning. But how would you feel if you found out that the orange tree that you once planted cannot bear any fruit at all? As the one who grew the tree, you must feel very disappointed about it.

How would you feel if you have not pursued your truest passion and dream? How would you feel if you reached your highest goal and ambition, but nobody has acknowledged or remembered you on the last days of your life? Have you ever made a difference in order to be remembered? Have you maximized your fullest potential? Have you made use of all your talents and skills to potentially inspire, in effect causing a positive change in other people's lives? These questions are driven to make you determine if your life is just for your personal gain or for others as well.

A person does not have to live a perfect and luxurious life to have or to discover his or her special purpose. In fact, most of the people who are so clear of their purpose are the ones who have experienced the lowest time of their lives. These are the people who can say, "I've been there and done that" with so much self-assurance and passion. Having "been there and done that," meaning going through the roller coaster of life, has given them the opportunity to reflect and ask why the experience has happened to them. It is having the ability to understand and absorb the learning from it, and after which, having to realize and find out what their mission is based on the particular episode of their lives.

It is not just important to be clear with your life's purpose, but to wholeheartedly accept the calling and of course to make it happen as well!

SELF-LEADERSHIP GUIDED WITH SPIRITUALITY

"Self-leadership is a pre-requisite to organizational leadership" (machetorres.com). How can a person manage to improve his/her personal relationship with others if he/she cannot make amends with oneself?

People with deep essence in life practice self-leadership. It is the propensity to govern the self, first, before others. It is having the natural ability to engage in retrospection and letting go of the painful past to be able to move forward, as well as to introspect and to learn to live in the moment in order to maximize one's capability and potential. In introspection, a person should be able to access and accept corresponding feelings and emotions in order to validate the situation for better understanding and troubleshooting.

Self-leadership is very important to leaders of any organization. The typical so-called 'heartless' leaders cannot naturally connect to their employees or subordinates due to a lack of self-awareness. It is a usual sign of the lack of self-confidence and inner strength. Due to this, it would be hard for him or her to show and feel compassion for others since there is lack of respect and of knowledge of oneself. Hence, it is important for an individual to lead oneself first before others.

Spirituality is an important ingredient for proper guidance in self-leadership. It is important to believe that there is always a Higher Power that helps you direct your life to the right path. It is the positive motivation that you need to look up to in order to assure yourself that you are doing the right thing and that you are making the right decisions in life.

STRENGTH WITHIN

Do you possess the inner strength that a person needs in order to surpass all of life's trials and tribulations? Are you malleable enough to bend with the storms of life and still have a clear vision of what must be achieved to solve a problem?

Inner strength promotes better understanding of the self. It is a result of having high self-worth and self-esteem. A person who has strengthened his / her inner foundation knows his or her truest worth. It is one of the main ingredients to self-leadership as well.

Achieving inner strength can be a long process for some. Have you ever met a person who may have an external facade of being strong, but in reality are quite vulnerable and weak on the inside? The facade or the person's mask is the person's natural defense mechanism to cover their true self. He or she lacks self-awareness, which contributes to their insecurity.

A person with genuine inner strength possesses his or her own individuality. In effect, he or she can easily determine his or her needs, goals, and purpose in life.

In achieving inner strength, it is necessary to learn how to reconnect with your inner child who needs to be nurtured. It is the process of unloading and forgiving your painful past, including yourself, who is the hardest person to forgive. Once the reconnection has been established, you need to learn to realize that you were made perfectly and lovably patterned in the image of your Creator.

ENVISION YOUR POWERFUL EXISTENCE

Do you have the ability to envision yourself making a difference in the universe? Do you see yourself empowered and doing the things that you are called to this world to do?

Having the skill to envision and to program a powerful existence is a prerequisite to success as well. It is the ability to create a clear vision of how you want your life to be in the future. Not just seeing it, but feeling it! Others may call it the "law of attraction," wherein what you perceive is what you receive. Hence, it shows how powerful the human mind is and how it influences our lives.

Negative thoughts and actions can easily dominate a person's energy and well-being. Many do not understand the ill effects of negativity in everyday life. It is usually triggered if a person has not unloaded or forgiven their painful past. His or her life is still covered with so much anger, guilt, and fear. All these past negative emotions can easily be carried on as baggage into the present, and operate unconsciously as negative programs in the future as well.

The importance of using the positive energies around you to work in your favor should be emphasized. In effect, it is a powerful way to easily dominate the negative forces around you. High spirituality is vital to help you enhance the virtues of faith, hope, and love. Faith that the best is yet to come; hope in the future; love for God, self, and others. In this process, do not underestimate the power of love, which is considered the strongest energy in the universe. Based on findings and experiences, love has been proven to heal in many different manifestations.

Having a crystal clear vision and ultimate feeling of your powerful existence gives you the chance to own your future successes and great endeavors.

NURTURE YOUR INNER CHILD

Do you think that you have reconnected with your inner child? Does your inner child feel nurtured, loved, accepted, assured, or even forgiven?

Have you ever experienced seeing glimpses of your childhood? Either seeing oneself happy or sad as a child? Most people have vivid memories of either their unhappy or happy childhood…

Regardless of your current age—you may be in your twenties or even in your eighties—you have a little child within you. The little child that you once were, that you need to face once again… to nurture, to love, to accept, to forgive and to assure.

How do you face this little child again? Most of the grownups with unhappy childhoods attempt to forcedly forget their traumatic experiences. In effect, they allow their unhappy childhoods to unconsciously affect the present and the future.

There is usually a natural tendency of creating a huge, high, and thick wall between yourself and your inner child. It is the defense mechanism consciously made to protect the present self from remembering the painful childhood experience as a whole.

Your inner child or your little one (who is the much younger you) may have experienced unthinkable trauma in the past. He or she may have experienced so much fear, anger, and guilt. But the problem started when as a child, you had confusion in processing your real feelings towards the experience. These negative feelings can only be made clear and acceptable to oneself once revisited and validated.

Your traumatized inner child may be a product of "old school" teachings; may have absorbed negative effects from social media; may have had a strict and conservative family and cultural background.

For example, a woman from an Asian culture during her younger years is made to believe that she is not deserving of respect, equal opportunities, and future success. She is sadly treated as a second-class citizen. Or for other cultures, children are not given the chance to express themselves. Children who have experienced a dictatorial upbringing have had their opinions and feelings suppressed early in life; hence, they lack self-confidence in their grownup years.

Sadly, in effect, they possess self-limiting beliefs. They become indecisive in choosing their future personal careers. For some, even after choosing a certain field, they still find it hard to excel. They lack self-awareness and cannot maximize their fullest potentials.

As a grownup, your assurance to your little one is very crucial. Reconnect with your inner child by putting him or her back at the core of your being where he or she truly belongs. Make your inner child feels safe and secure inside of you. Unload the negative emotions that your inner child once had and learn from it. A firm assurance and forgiveness will create a strong bond between the two of you. Always be there to love and nurture your inner child!

COMPASSIONATE SOUL

Do you consider yourself as a being with a compassionate soul? Do you have the ability to empathize with others? Do you give others the benefit of the doubt or just judge other people?

A person with a compassionate soul has a genuine ability to connect. It is usually the skill of having a natural "soul to soul" connection with another person. He or she does not notice the physical attributes—i.e., color, gender, race, etc.—but instead sees through the inner being of the other person. With this method, a person may feel that he or she has known the person for a long time.

A person with a compassionate soul is sensitive to the needs of others as well, even before it is asked of them. It is one of the hardest virtues to possess. It is sad that some people will have to go through life's proving before they feel empathy for others. People who cannot feel for or empathize with others have the natural tendency of judging. Hence, the universe would automatically let them go through the same experience just to give them a better understanding of the situation.

If you consider yourself to have a compassionate soul, then it will be much less effortless for you to assess your real essence and purpose. It is when you have the genuine initiative to do something to make a difference in this lifetime.

EMBRACE CHANGE WITH EXTREME GRATITUDE

The Change

Have you ever been rattled by a life-changing event in your life? Did you unconditionally embrace the change, or frantically blame the universe for letting you experience it?

Embracing change during the lowest point of a person's life can be very challenging. Imagine being stripped of your life's comforts and stability. It is the ability to acknowledge and to accept that the change is happening right in front of your eyes. The blinders that create denial of the situation must be taken off! Somehow, it is always difficult to grasp the essence of the drastic big change until we understand all of the things that were discussed earlier:

- E - mpowered Existence with a Deep Purpose
- S - elf Leadership Guided with Spirituality
- S - trength Within
- E - nvision Your Powerful Existence
- N - urture Your Inner Child
- C - ompassionate Soul

and, E - for embracing the change with extreme gratitude, which completes the truest essence of your existence.

Extreme gratitude is when you can look back to thank everyone who has participated in the big change, including the ones who have hurt you. It is an ultimate recognition to your truest essence, signifying a firm foundation of your existence. It is being triumphant after going through life's trials and tribulations, proving that you, as a victorious survivor, can now easily go through life with ease!

This reminds me of our fellow Filipinos in Tacloban who have survived the aftereffects of Typhoon Haiyan (Yolanda) in

November 2013. The majority of the population lost their homes, families, and livelihood. It has been over two years now and most of them have not yet fully recovered. Their resilience and inner strength have inspired most of us Filipinos.

Our Rotary Club had the chance to visit Tacloban months ago to install water filtration units in various public schools that do not have clean water systems. I would say that the local businessmen, some of whom are fellow Rotarians from that district, have proven their deepest commitment to help out their province. They had the option to move out and to start all over somewhere else, but instead they decided to stay to create businesses and to help create more jobs for the survivors. They have simply proven their essence of existence. May God bless their purest hearts!

My Personal Reflection

I would like to personally dedicate this chapter to my late father, Jaime T. Torres, who inspired and taught me to be the person that I am right now. I vividly remember when I whispered my last message to him on his deathbed, "Papa thank you for everything! Thank you for all the love, care, and learning in life! I appreciate all the material wealth that you have left us, but the real legacy that I need from you is your inner strength and wisdom ... please continue to guide me..."

My father was not just a self-made man who had reached the peak of his career and success both as an educator and as a businessman, but was somebody who realized his truest essence early in his life's journey. His philanthropic deeds to give back to society has changed and helped a lot of people's lives. Being a private school owner and co-founder with my mother, he educated hundreds of scholars who have graduated with a quality education. They will always be grateful to him and their success is one of his greatest legacies!

In exploring the deepest essence of your existence, learn that the quality of your life depends on your deep understanding of your purpose. Be an instrument to inspire others. Maximize and enhance your capabilities, strengths, talents, and wisdom. Accept the calling and just do what you are meant to do in this lifetime!

***

To Contact Mache:

Website: www.machetorres.com

Email: machetorres412@yahoo.com

SKYPE: mache888

VIBER: 639175940412

Mindy Anderson

Certified Business and Life Coach.

Mindy is a recognized sales leader, speaker, trainer, co-author, and GO GETTER! She has built three successful Sales and Marketing organizations. Mindy hosts and trains at training seminars. She previously held the position of International Advisory Board member of a Relationship Marketing Company.

Mindy has worked in the capacity of Stock Broker-Priority Shareholder Rep., Production Specialist, sales assistant, office manager, International tour guide, bookkeeper, insurance & annuity agent, and real estate agent!! Her favorite title is Mom and Mimi.

What some have said about her trainings: "Love your style of training"; "You deserve big kudos, I love the sincere professionalism. Not a bunch of fast hype"; "Enjoyed your presentation and directness."

When she isn't working, her main passion is hiking and camping through the mountains with her family.

Lead Yourself First Before You Lead Others

Mindy Anderson

Life Sucks!! Nothing I do works!! I was depressed, I had a bad attitude, and I did not feel good about myself. I was bitter, had no hope of things ever being better, and everything was a struggle. Life was a bummer. I was on the struggle bus!

I had been a person that allowed life to happen to me. I always reacted. I didn't make big goals or plans. Everything just came to me, then I would decide. There was no proactive planning. The realization of choosing a life I wanted instead of a random life that just happens was startling. I remember hearing friends talk about planning for their children and planning education to get specific careers. This was a mental challenge for me. I didn't do that! All planning for education was shelved because I had two children by age 21 and survival was in high gear. The big recession of the 1980s was upon us and planning was not a luxury I had at that time. We were broke! I lived my life by taking care of my children and just barely getting by.

Many years later, I remember vividly the exact moment the thought occurred to me, *you must control your mind and your thoughts*. The next thought was, *oh my gosh, that is going to be so… hard*!! It's true. It is hard.

I had a real faith in God, but life wasn't working. Everything was a struggle. If you want change and are sincere, I believe it comes. It may be slow, but I believe it comes as long as you are persistently pursuing change. I needed a change. In fact, *I* needed to change.

I started hearing messages from teachers/preachers and various people about thankfulness and being grateful. I heard a message about offering a sacrifice of praise to God. Wow—talk about thought provoking! It was hard. I wanted to hold on to my anger. I had been wronged. This was just the beginning for me.

I began to be thankful and look at what I had instead of what I didn't have. I had a picture in my mind of a giant watermill or waterwheel that was slowly beginning to turn. Isn't it interesting that waterwheels create energy! My mind began to think differently. I began to see that I had a bad attitude. Messages were coming at me and I began to absorb the right ones. I read books on personal development. My mind was transforming. I began to own my own stuff! This never happens quickly. The person I was took years to develop and the new person was taking years to change. The biggest part of this is the fact that I wanted this change. I was sick of myself!

In my corporate job, I was able to take a course called "Leading Yourself." Then I took the next course, "Leading Yourself with Mastery." At first, when I began to write down statements of "I will," I was very skeptical. I thought it was so cheesy. It hit me after approximately a year that what I had written "I will" for was actually happening. For example, I said "I will have Sunday dinner with my kids" and I did!

Everything I read was with caution and skepticism. It was a challenge for my mind to switch over so quickly. This was good, though, as it caused me to wrestle with it in my mind and emotions so that ultimately I was becoming stronger. I was choosing my new thoughts.

Fatalism is the belief that all things are predetermined to occur and there is no ability to alter this predetermined plan. You hear people say, "It is God's will" or "it is the way it is" or "it must be my destiny". Sometimes it is true, but of course many times it is not true. We have power to plan and change things. Modern medicine is full of examples of choices you can make to take control and improve your life. The examples of mere human beings that change the course of the world is well proven.

I believed in fate, not destiny. Destiny was something you could affect by the choices you made. Simple choices are easy. Going to college with the intention of a chosen career was not an option I ever saw I had. College and planning out life was not discussed in my childhood. My parents were Depression-era children and they each came from broken homes where they learned to make choices to survive. For me, too, it was only about surviving and having fun along the way. This was not a thriving life, but an existence.

Do you remember when the book *The Purpose Driven Life* by Rick Warren came out? I found this book to be incredible. To me, this was another thought-provoking opportunity. Actually having a purpose! Living with a plan! Planning and choosing. This was leading myself to what I wanted to accomplish and think about who I was. It seemed out of my league, out of my grasp.

Every step along the slow waterwheel journey was preparing me to become better and be intentional; I was learning to lead myself. I was becoming awake, aware, and alive; I was learning to live with intention!

You either believe in fatalism, which is minimal control in life, or you believe that YOU can change your life and you have power. I must say first that I believe this is very true for most of us. I also believe there are places in the world where it is far more complicated to make choices and lead an intentional life due to government and religion. However, I learned from my reading that even in prison, a person who has almost zero control can control their mind and attitude. I was challenged by a quote I read from Viktor Frankl: "The one thing you can't take away from me is the way I choose to respond to what you do to me. The last of one's freedoms is to choose one's attitude in any given circumstance." Frankl was an Austrian neurologist and psychiatrist, as well as a Holocaust survivor. Dr. Frankl, also said, "A human being is a deciding being."

Think about the people who have changed this world. Jesus Christ changed the world with only 12 disciples. Winston Churchill is another one of my favorites. What many people don't realize about Churchill is that he was considered a failure for some of his elite life. Yet he was brave and courageous in his beliefs. Churchill was famous for his stubborn resistance to Hitler during the worst times in WWII. He stood alone in his beliefs many times and was told he was through in his political career. We all know what a challenge it is to want everyone to "like" you or to all agree or just get along.

Lincoln was such a man to be self-taught and very determined to lead by what he believed to be the right and true way to lead others. He became one of the greatest Presidents in history. He led himself according to his beliefs and convictions. You and I can truly change the world if we know we can and if we want to. It may not be as grand as the ones I mentioned, but what about our children and community? Even the smallest determination can lead to great change for ourselves and others.

Let's not forget the great women too, like Margaret Thatcher, Britain's first female prime minister, who was pivotal in British and world politics. She had strong self-leadership. She once stood up at the Conservative party conference and stated: "You turn if you want to, but this lady is not for turning." This was characteristic of her—extremely strong in her beliefs and commitment.

The Change[10]

Napoleon Hill proclaimed, "Successful people make decisions quickly and firmly. Unsuccessful people make decisions slowly, and they change them often." This quote really impacted me. I have been a person that would waffle based on the better argument. I asked myself, "what do I believe?" Based on my faith, conviction, and current state of mind, what do I believe?

It is most important to know who you are and what you believe. To be firm in belief and action until convinced otherwise. As I became firm in my beliefs, my decisions and actions became stronger and more cohesive. Using my belief system was helping me to make better decisions and I was choosing a plan for my future. I was leading myself; not being led.

Here are some excellent statements that cause thought and action:

Be clear about what you are doing.

Have a definite purpose - Be definite.

Discouragement comes from not being clear. Take courageous, confident action.

Who am I, where am I going? Ask: Does this move me to what I want?

Thoughts are things and have energy. People are attracted to courage.

Fate or life hit me so many times, and each time it moved me in a new direction. It was as if I was a leaf blowing in the wind. I cannot say I was in complete mental awareness. I moved based on the choices at hand. I was just accepting fate; I was choosing because of fate. In my 30's, I made BIG changes. Then at the age of 42, I made another huge choice for my future. I took control. I chose to leave my career because of my child's illness. This was not easy. I had to find a way to make an income working from home. I had never done that before!

I have found many people that are faced with a difficult decision or a decision made for them (fate), like being fired or laid off, who actually thrive and find something new and more rewarding, even if the struggle lasted for years. I believe the ones that were happiest refused bitterness and moved on. That is what happened to me. I chose Multi-level Marketing to bring in an income. I was so scared; I had never done anything like this before and I knew nothing about the industry.

There was so much self-examination, striving to find people, and saying the right words. Trying to balance and to captivate the right ones to join me was exhausting at the beginning. Every new growth is exhausting when you try to master a thing. Despite my fear, I was leading myself on wobbly legs.

Self-sabotage can be a close cousin to leading yourself. Personal growth usually is three steps forward and one back with a continual upward curve, meaning you can backslide to old levels of comfort. I recently found myself depressed and unable to be in total alignment with mastering myself. I was weak and everything I was experiencing was ticking me off. It seemed like it was layering up. I wasn't sure if it was a force within me wanting to change and move in a new direction or if I was self-sabotaging. These two are so parallel. I knew I really needed to isolate myself and begin to ask myself what was going on and to journal. I was struck with the knowledge that I was not leading myself. I was reacting to things being placed in front of me for decisions. As I was looking and making decisions, I was also being distracted from what my true objective was. I was no longer focused. I was focusing on too many things. Therefore, I was weak and not performing at peak level. My change came when I re-examined my main objective and what

The Change

method I would take to achieve that objective. I realized I needed to make the decision to quit being distracted and focus in once again.

I made some decisions that I thought would be tough, but they were necessary and easy because I made a strong decision based on my main objective. I was firm. I was going in one direction until I no longer could go any other way. I had to face the fact that ego and pride were allowing me to be distracted. Honesty with yourself is the only way to make right choices. This honesty could now be identified as self-sabotage. Another new level of growth was happening. It is always painful as we grow, isn't it? We must choose continual growth; it doesn't just happen. Not being honest with yourself can cause mistakes.

I read a statement from Dr. John C. Maxwell. He stated that during a Q&A session at a conference, someone asked, "What has been your greatest challenge as a leader?" "Leading me!" he answered. "That has always been my greatest challenge as a leader." He said something else so funny, "If I could kick the person responsible for my problems, I wouldn't be able to sit down for a week!"

I felt so much better about myself. I was in great company! If Dr. John C. Maxwell can understand this and admit it, then so can I. I was not struggling with this for nothing; I struggle because I am about to break free! This is an affirmation that I am on the right track and am aware something is wrong and it has a name. I have been dancing around this subject without even knowing it and now the time had come to CHANGE!

If you have read or heard something and it sticks with you and bothers you, then it comes again and again, it is your time to wrestle it down—to master the thought and make a decision on it.

How many times have you heard of Rock and Roll bands falling apart because of ego and pride? Of course they don't call it ego and pride, they say a disagreement or falling out. The incredibly talented Steve Jobs was kicked out of his own company. His choice was clear, fate hit him, and he made decisions based on that incident. These challenges force us to change or move into another direction, but it always calls for introspection of our attitude and decisions. Sometimes we make decisions based on others, like kids, spouse, family, or ourselves! My decision to leave my career was based on my child. I could have hired a nanny or gotten help from others, but the logical decision was to take care of her myself. This pushed me, based on my decision, to find an alternate way to make a living at home. The trick is to NOT second-guess your decision. You might lament that you could have been the Director or the CEO by now, but you made a decision based on current circumstances and you must move forward and not lament. It is done. If you handle it this way, you can save yourself so much agony of "what if". Own your decision. Embrace it. Let it move you to new places. If it was wrong, own it as new knowledge in order to not make the same mistake again.

Have you ever heard anyone say, "You are the cause of your own problems"? How about this one, "Everything happens for a reason, sometimes the reason is you're stupid and make bad decisions"! I love it! It is true. So many times, the problems we have are of our own making. No one will ever be perfect and we must make mistakes in order to learn. Embracing this truth; no longer blaming others and becoming bitter is key. Does bitterness serve you? NEVER! Bitterness never serves us. This is where making firm decisions comes into play. Let's say you work for a company that you really like. The owner makes a bad move that affects your paycheck. You get many people you work with that begin to gripe and complain. You are mad too. Their complaints and your own personal feelings and thoughts are fueling your anger. Your boss doesn't return your call or email and you are ALONE and becoming bitter and angrier all the time. Does this feeling and attitude help? NO!

Another quote that has helped me overcome bitterness and anger is from Socrates: "What screws us up most in life is the picture in our head of how it is supposed to be."

In my scenario of the boss making bad decisions that affect you, of course your boss will make mistakes! You will too! The picture in our head wants perfection. Heaven will be perfection. Change the picture while here on earth. Allowing for reality in our picture will help all relationships.

Your words and actions will create energy that will create harmony for a state of mind that will influence and attract others. What you say (word), do (actions), and think (thoughts) need to be in harmony. This is where leading yourself becomes power—energy—influential—attractive. People may or may not follow you, but they will respect the fact that you believe and are all-in on what you are doing.

Have you ever met a person that pitches you on one thing and if you don't bite, they pitch you on something else? There is no harmony in this. No true leadership. It happens quite a bit in Multi-level Marketing.

It has taken me years to grow to where I am today. I was not ready for the early messages I received. However, the seeds were planted and were there, ready to grow when the time was right. Growth is a journey that once started rewards greatly. I am always so impatient with myself. Not every message is for you and sometimes it is not for you at the time, but when it is time, you will wrestle until you achieve it if you choose to.

***

To Contact Mindy:

elimsprings3@gmail.com

www.facebook.com/bizcoach4winds

Pamela Hamilton and W.T. Hamilton

Pamela Hamilton and W.T. Hamilton are the authors of the amazing, transformational book series *Your Invincible Power* and they are expanding the possibility of next through their Success Coaching. This mother and son team bring a unique voice to self-empowerment. They have written five motivational books, inspiring readers to ignite their ambition and accelerate their success. Written to somewhat abate the concept and limited views of the world's opinion of limitation in wealth, health, and joy, they guide the reader, using easy to use exercises and techniques. Based on many of their own life experiences, they enlighten their audience and give them tools to live the life they have longed for.

Each author approaches Your Invincible Power and discovering your inner strength in a way that complements the other, but also defines their individuality. Pamela works with these powers in a more spiritual mind, connecting to universal energies, theories, and philosophies. W.T. engages more with the logical mind, using practical applications, tests, and actions. The two have been called an unlikely duo, but the end result is a full comprehension of the what, why, and how this great gift works, and can work, for all those who welcome it.

Warning, Take a Deep Breath

You're About to Learn How to Make the Impossible Possible

By Pamela and W.T. Hamilton

Think for a moment: where would you like to go if you could go anywhere in the world right now? Think about what that experience would feel like. Think about what it would sound like. Now think about who would be there with you. See their face, their smile, and their joy. What are the sounds around you? What are the scents? How does it feel to experience this? Hold that thought in your mind for a moment. Really think about this experience. See the details of this experience in your mind. Think about how wonderful it is to do this, the feeling of freedom in doing it, and the feeling of accomplishment that accompanies the experience. Build it in your mind as a memory of an experience you have already lived.

Now I want you to intend to experience it in the future. I want you to promise yourself that you will live this experience at some point in your future. I want you to visit this place you just created often, throughout the day, in the stolen moments and daydreams of your life. This is the beginning of building your successful life. This is the beginning of creating your future life—your dream life.

It is with intent that anything becomes something. It is with the intent to succeed that you become successful. It is born within, in thought, before it can be experienced. It is this invincible power that you already possess that will enable you to manifest your dreams and goals.

This exercise will give you a place to go to—a goal that is not defined by how much money you make or how big your house is, but by the experiences that you create and the memories that you live. It is how you build your dream life. But building your dream is often a misunderstood process that brings mediocre results because the purpose of being successful didn't include the intent of being successful. Instead of intent, it is replaced with a hope or a wish. But a hope or a wish comes from the mind of doubt; it is from the place where unsuccessful people congregate to complain about how unfair life is. This is not intent; this is not becoming successful on purpose. This is becoming successful by accident or by luck. Unfortunately, this way is not repeatable, and many may not even realize they reached their goal because they weren't sure what their goal really looked like.

If your goal is to be rich, what does rich look like? How much money will you need to have before you feel successful? If your goal is to be famous, how famous is famous? You see, becoming successful on purpose begins with defining your definition of success. It is a critical step that most people never set foot on. The idea of what success looks like is not created by them, but is instead inherited, leaving the power of intent in someone else's hands. But this is your dream or goal, so why should they define your definition of achieving it?

When you inherit the definition of success, it is defined by your status, address, career, and net worth. But this is really the fruit of your success, nothing more. Success is simply achieving something you set out to do. Your definition of success should be of things that are only important to you and that make you feel happy, excited, and satisfied. You should know what your success looks like. It should be things that you want to achieve and experience. When we base our goals on an experience, there is a clear and easy way to picture it and know when it manifests. This is where the power of intent takes hold. So what is the power of intent?

That which you desire to experience or have will only come to you through creating the outcome over and over again in your thought. *It is known as thinking on purpose.* The thought that is held in the mind backward and forward, day and night, conscious and subconscious, will come to be the experiences that make up your life.

When we add intent to our desire or goal, we give it an energy that magnetizes it. It is thinking on purpose about the goal or desire that manifests the conditions to create the experience of success. It is your invincible power and you have access to it at all times. It begins in the thinking of a goal, desire, or dream life; seeing what the experience looks like; and keeping that picture in your mind for as many moments as possible throughout the day. But this is one of the hurdles of success. Our mind often wants to explore new thoughts. It doesn't naturally hold the same thought for long periods of time unless it is something unpleasant that brings emotions of fear or failure. Only negative thoughts seem to play in our mind without cease.

But what if you could learn to stay focused on a goal, any goal, until it was achieved, no matter how long it takes? How do we keep the same goal on our mind day in and day out for an unlimited duration of time?

Success begins with believing you can succeed at what you are focused on. It is in the focusing that you are able to draw the opportunities, resources, and ambition to reach your goals. It is in the mind of having that your dreams manifest. But before you can put this into action, before you can focus on what you want, you have to develop your inner strength: your invincible power.

It is in building this inner strength that you will be able to build the belief that you can reach whatever goal you are focused on. It is thinking with intent that will enable you to manifest what you see in your mind. But if that is the case, then why do so many people fail? What is stopping everyone from believing they can manifest their dreams?

It Is the Egoic Mind

How much do you really know about your ego? How much of this hidden entity is actually directing your life to a journey you would rather not take?

Yes, you're right, this sounds quite ridiculous if you have never really thought about the ego. Regardless, this part of your personality is at the forefront of every choice you make. The problem is, until you recognize it and learn how to make choices independently, it will always be there guiding you the wrong way.

So what is this ego and how does it work in our lives?

This is a way you can tell how the ego is working in your decision-making:

Ask yourself, "Will the result of this choice I am making have any harmful repercussions for me or anyone else if I implement this choice?" If the heartfelt feeling is benevolent for not only you, but for those affected, life is showing to you the right decision. However, if that decision brings any anxiety or if you fret, agonize, or lose sleep over it, you know without a doubt that it is not only the wrong decision, but also that your ego is involved in your decision-making, nudging you along to make the wrong choice.

Throughout each moment of our day, we are making choices, mostly very small choices; nevertheless, they come at us constantly. The voice in our head just doesn't stop. Insignificant choices are, "Should I have a cinnamon bun or a carrot muffin?" Major choices in comparison would be, "Should I tell my best friend her husband is cheating on her?" The ego would definitely try to convince you that the latter choice is right. You see, the egoic mind is that part of you that pushes you into the negative field.

The next question would be, "Why do we have a part of us that would like us to fail in life?"

We have been given a vast amount of circumstances, situations, and incidents through our lifetime that are all set up in polarities. Most of these we consider to be either good or bad, positive or negative, light or dark, and so forth. All of this is set up by a mighty universe for our benefit. This dualism gives us selection. If there were no polarities, there would be no choice. Life would have no meaning. The ego was activated through ambiguity, to give more value to choice, to be adept at swiftly evaluating all situations, and then quickly coming to the conclusion of what you most want. In other words, the egoic mind was set up to make us conscious of the negative part of that choice—to nudge us, without fear, into a positive solution. The ego had not yet become our adversary. This all changed when a few patronizing men introduced fear in the 6th through 13th centuries (which is now widely known as the Dark Ages.) It was a tumultuous period where conscious thought gave way to manipulation. And belief in being in control of our own destination had been laid to rest.

Once fear was introduced, it changed the egoic mind. Fear became its prime priority. Fear comes from negative self-talk that reiterates many nullifying messages that may leave you feeling contemptible, inferior, and insignificant, among many other hurtful blows this nasty memorandum delivers to our psyche. All of this leaves us feeling unworthy. The ego maneuvers through negative thoughts only. It has lots of leeway, and it operates through our subconscious.

The substance we furnish our minds with is what the ego has learned to use to deliver negative pressure.

We are first introduced to fear as children. Once doubt and fear are presented to us, the ego is able to use its power. Without doubt and fear, the ego would sink into the depth of our thoughts, no longer holding any power; instead, it would just be there to gently nudge us on: the reason it was created in the first place. The way things stand now, the ego is our antagonist only because we have been vulnerable in allowing it to run our thoughts. When things are fear based, the ego is able to deceive us by injecting uncertainty in our decision-making. So through the ages, we have learned to live from unworthiness through fear because we can't possibly be manipulated any other way. The way out of this is by consciously making choices that benefit us. If we are able to see through this undesirable part of us, we can learn how to change it.

The Birth of this Assailant

Parents are anxiously keeping their children safe and emphasize the dangers that surround them. All of this lurches in the dark recesses of their mind and stresses the child through fear. This is how the influential ego affects us negatively.

There is no reason to blame parents, nor their ancestors. Let's face it, we have to keep our children safe. However, if parents make sure their children are as safe as they can possibly be without fear and stress and without uttering constantly what could possibly happen to the child, the child would be safeguarded from major fear. The child, without a doubt, would not generate the fear of their parents.

To counteract this thought process, we have to replace those messages of unworthiness with messages that inspire us. We have to take control of our life by understanding that all we want to see can and will take place if we believe in our own abilities. We are not at the mercy of a loveless world that only wants us to fail—only wants us to flounder and falter. This is not why we are here. This universe is a loving, compassionate universe that only gives out joy. We are the only obstacle in our way, not some element or entity that we may perceive to be against us at every turn in the road. These are mere thoughts that we have processed over time.

Thoughts and the Subconscious Mind

Through the manipulation of centuries and through no fault of our own, we have lost the ability to utilize the power of thought. We are working from a primitive concept. The concepts we live by are that thoughts are only a puff of air that dissipate the moment they leave our mind. The truth is that thoughts are very powerful, and the more concentration the thought holds, the more that thought will turn into reality. In other words, our lives take direction from our thoughts, so if you live with negative thoughts and worry constantly, you will draw more of that negativity into your life. Regardless, if you live with positive thoughts, then life will bring forth wonderful situations, people, and places. This happens through your subconscious mind. And our subconscious mind works through the mighty law of attraction. The law of attraction says "That which is like unto itself is drawn," and so whatever you are focused on eventually sinks into your subconscious mind and eventually draws to it that which you have been preoccupied with.

The Power of Inner Strength

The power of inner strength says, "All that you need to feel joy and happiness, love and belonging, compassion and harmony, is already within you. It comes from internal and manifests external. It comes from within and can only be achieved from within."

Whatever you give your attention to, possibly a repeated negative memory, or a negative situation you are drawn into, or it could be a project that you do not want to contemplate but you feel you must, there are numerous scenarios you could possibly activate. The actual framework of these concepts are under your control through your thoughts because whatever you deliberately focus on will change for your own benefit. By deliberately seeing the object of attention as being positive, even delightful, you will see the changes that you want to manifest. The negative situations will also dissolve into the background of your life along with the egoic mind.

So as you are able to recognize when the egoic mind is at play, you can gain control over it and bring your focus to the life you deserve. No longer will the voice of the egoic mind discourage you. Instead, the vision of your inner strength will encourage you and inspire you to reach for the goal or desire that plays in your mind.

Your inner strength is an invincible power that will allow you to connect to your goals and dreams. As you begin to think with intent, you begin to load your subconscious mind with the images and messages that will become a part of your thinking pattern over time. As you gain control over the egoic mind and fuel your subconscious with messages of belief and achieving, with images of the experience you will have, you start to change your energy alignment and are creating the mind of having. This will be a powerful evolution for you. It is at this time that you begin to write your own future.

This is how success is manifested. This is how ideas become things. It is with the power of intent and the power of inner strength. It is in building the belief that you will experience the picture that you have created in your mind. It is knowing that this picture has already been experienced in great detail, in thought, and it will come to be in the now of yesterday's tomorrow. It is with the consistent loading of the subconscious mind that the experience becomes indistinguishable as a past or future memory and will come to be a manifestation.

So your assignment is to add great detail to the images that you created at the beginning of this chapter. You will need to set aside 5-10 uninterrupted minutes in the morning, before the demands and chaos of the day welcome you, and think on purpose about the experience you created, as you did in the beginning of this chapter. You will need to visit this experience for a few moments throughout the day. At night, after you have closed your tablet, laptop, and smartphone, give yourself another 5-10 uninterrupted minutes to get lost in the memory of the experience. Continue this exercise for the next 21 days; this will load your subconscious and begin to draw the opportunities to you to manifest this goal, dream, or desire into the now.

Through this chapter, life has presented you with a choice. You are reading this because life wants you to move forward with joy and give you all of your desires. Do not be fooled that it is selfish to have all that you want. The universe is not stingy; if you observe nature, there is nothing that isn't overflowing with abundance. A great fire can burn all vegetation for thousands of miles, and within time, that same vegetation will flow with abundance once again. Life is showing us constantly that all of what we desire is ours once we believe. This abundance is our invincible power to claim. Allow the ego to do its original job: to nudge you on in your decision-making without fear.

We wish you joy, love, and all the abundance that your heart desires.

***

To Contact Pamela and W.T.

www.yourinvinciblepower.com

https://www.facebook.com/yourinviciblepower

https://twitter.com/w_t_hamilton

https://www.selfgrowth.com/experts/wt-pamela-hamilton

success@yourinviciblepower.com

Neil Millard

Neil Millard is a successful business owner, entrepreneur, speaker, and coach. He is passionate about personal development and awareness. As a trained coach in Broadband Consciousness and other disciplines, Neil uses his own experiences and training to help others on their journey through quietening the civil war in people's minds and teaching methods to get financial stability.

Having spent many years in the financial sector with clients such as Barclays, Lloyds, and AXA, he is now on a mission to share his wide sphere of financial knowledge with the world. Neil has seen all sides of the personal and business financial spectrum—from bankruptcy to business ownership—so he draws on a great pool of expertise.

Neil is also a keen philanthropist, a passion he channels by directing HEARTS Global, which supports many projects around the world—from sponsoring schoolchildren in Sri Lanka to raising literacy levels for adult learners in the UK.

And, of course, Neil is well known as the wizard of technical infrastructures and assists businesses embrace new technology such as the cloud to move faster, become more agile, and better respond to their customers' wants and needs.

What BC Did For Me

By Neil Millard

Throughout my life, I have experienced highs and lows. It has taken me a long time to come to terms with some of the events from my past and to use them positively. I owe much of this to my partner, Wendy, and to two very important influencers, Richard and Liz, who opened my eyes and helped me discover and achieve my purpose: to contribute, to grow, and to be content. I want to share this gift with you on your journey through life.

Let's begin with my beginning:

I was born to my parents David and Wendy in 1975. A year later, my little sister joined us. Another big change for our family that year was Dad joining the RAF, which meant lots of moving around and before the age of nine, I had already been lucky enough to live in Cyprus, Germany, and the UK. Some children find this constant state of transition difficult, and perhaps it has affected me as an adult, but at nine years old, I thrived on it: I was at the top of my classes, I had good friends, and was the leader of a small gang influenced by Lee Majors—an actor popular for his portrayal of a stuntman moonlighting as a bounty hunter in *The Fall Guy*. We would play pranks, have play fights, and become stuntmen (until teatime, of course). I had access to a ZX81 computer and started a lifelong passion for computer programming. In short, life was good.

Then, when I was ten, my parents divorced. Many things changed.

My mum moved my sister and I to the council estate where my grandmother's house was. Rather than an exciting life moving around the world, I was now confined to a small house in a brand new area with no immediate prospect of escape. I missed my dad terribly. My bed-wetting, which I had never "grown out of," worsened and as a result I became self-conscious and didn't make friends as easily as before. I had further problems with my bladder and bowels and so had special treatment from the school staff, which wasn't always popular with my peers. All I wanted at that age was to blend in, but the extra attention meant quite the opposite happened. I earned the nickname "Smelly" at school and I became isolated. In hindsight, I was lonely, but at the time, I lost myself in computer programming—and listening to Kylie Minogue in my bedroom.

At 13, I moved to upper school and found some acceptance in four "fellow geeks"—a friendship circle that I still enjoy and am very grateful for today. This improved things for me and I started to gain an interest in girls. But there was a problem: I was still bed-wetting and there was a voice in my head telling me that no girl would ever want to be close with someone as smelly and nasty as me. I never asked a girl out, although I now wish I had. I recently bumped into a girl I had really liked at school and she said: "I still can't fathom why you never asked me out."

Life continued with its highs and lows; looking back, I can remember consistently following the plan that my parents had set out before me—go to school; get a job; meet a girl; get married and have a baby—because, according to my parents, their parents, and parents all the way back through the ages, this was the way to do it. It's easy to blame our parents, but ultimately they didn't know any better and can't inform your experience beyond their own. I knew I wasn't happy, despite adhering to the plan, but I continued to do all these expected things. I got several jobs, I went to college, I met a girl and married her, and she quickly became pregnant with our first daughter, Melissa.

The Change[10]

Around 25 weeks into the pregnancy, we took a trip to visit my brothers-in-law. My wife began bleeding on the way and we spent our week's holiday in Crawley Hospital. She was very ill and had to have an emergency caesarean. Sadly, Melissa did not survive and we never got to meet her whilst she was alive. What struck me the most at that tragic time was the huge loss of potential: who Melissa might have become, the things I could have taught her, experiences we might have had as a family. We had the funeral a week later.

We tried to get our lives back on an even keel after this; I returned to work and we became pregnant again. My daughter was born two weeks early in September 1999. It was a difficult pregnancy and another caesarean birth to endure, but our daughter was (and is) perfect.

Around the same time, I was offered redundancy and took it. The company that had forced the redundancy then recruited me at a higher salary. For the next four years, our family grew together. We enjoyed parenthood and family life, even with the occasional well-meant intervention from the in-laws.

Then I was offered redundancy again, this time without the immediate promise of another job. Although I was frustrated, it also meant I had more time to focus on a business I was then trying to get off the ground. It never did, and financial troubles loomed. I took contracting work, which meant I was away during the week and back with my family on weekends. I enjoyed spending my free time with my daughter whilst my wife was working over the weekends—an arrangement that suited us both well as the marriage had problems. Our debts were still building in spite of how hard we were both working and the sacrifices we made, putting a strain on the marriage and, shortly after I moved back permanently for a start of a new contract in Bristol, the relationship broke down altogether. I moved in with one of my sisters; and divorce was filed. I missed my daughter, but the divorce was the right decision for us and it felt like a fresh start. I remember getting some support from my mum, but it felt hollow somehow and I have since learnt to provide that support to and for myself.

The contract ended and nothing else was available. I was broke, divorced, missing my daughter, and felt unemployable. I relied on the support of my friends and the occasional work contract, but the books still wouldn't balance. Things seemed pretty hopeless.

Then I met a lovely lady called Wendy. With her love and encouragement, I finally settled into a permanent job. Wendy helped me to see a light at the end of the tunnel of my finances: I filed for bankruptcy and was really able to start afresh. Had I continued to strive to pay these debts off, I may never have done so and probably would have driven myself mad in the process. An unfortunate outcome of the bankruptcy was that everyone had to leave the family home. There were concerns over my daughter's health, too, which led to Children's Services involvement and an interview with the relevant teams was set. After two years, they eventually decided that her interests would be best met in foster care.

The week of the (as it turned out, pivotal) Children's Services meeting coincided with a booking I had made onto a "Broadband Consciousness" week, so I cancelled the seminar and attended a month later. This, it's fair to say, changed the way I looked on my past, my present, and my future; it gave me some new options for handling life. It also helped me to see that my results-driven, achieving nature had negatives as well as positives and that the good feelings I was working so hard for were in fact within easy reach without all the "things" I had previously seen as an integral part of the way to happiness. It helped me form concrete ideas about my purpose, and the importance of having a purpose in life.

The Change[10]

Our purpose is ultimately to be content, to grow, and to contribute. We also have a responsibility—to be aware of the impact your own actions have on others.

"Content" may seem like an odd choice of word—many self-help books might state that "delighted" or "ecstatic" are the ideal. Anyone who has been truly happy or crushingly sad, however, will be able to say how exhausting both these extremes states of being are to maintain. By contrast, contentment means that we are generally happy and fulfilled in our lives; we are therefore able to handle the extreme highs and lows of life events and to regain our equilibrium once those events have passed, leaving with us only their positive lessons.

Given the choice, most would choose to have a happy life rather than a sad one. We may have challenges that we face and overcome, we might be given fewer easy chances than someone else, but as we see in our discussion about Attitude, even though these things are often out of our control, we can choose the way we receive them.

We can sometimes be derailed from our contentment by

Internal forces such as what we feel we should do

External forces

Advertising and marketing

Chances

Catastrophe

You have probably heard many people use the phrase "I'll be happy when..." Maybe you've used it yourself, too, and it may seem a harmless, human desire to have more. And it can be very positive to push oneself to achieve...so long as you're happy whilst you're achieving.

"I'll be happy when..." is putting a time constraint on your happiness; you're not allowing yourself to be happy until you get "there" and have achieved your new girlfriend, boyfriend, house, job, car, etc. Advertisers will play on this and try to encourage you to get that product, that "happy factor," as soon as possible.

But most people never realize that they could be that happy right now! Consider the example below, keeping in mind what truly triggers our feelings:

The Car

Sandip has always wanted a VW Golf. He works two jobs, doesn't have any expensive hobbies, and saves up enough money until he can afford his car. Sandip is happy.

Jeremy has been advised that the company car contract has ended and the company is moving to a cheaper supplier in order to cut costs and avoid making redundancies. He will soon be getting a new company car. *Great*, thinks Jeremy, *I've always wanted a Jaguar*. The new car is delivered. It's a VW Golf. Jeremy is not pleased.

Surely, if cars make us happy, then both men should, by all accounts, be equally happy. They have received a car—exactly the same car, in fact. Could it be that the car, then, is not the "happy factor" after all?

Sandip feels he has earned a reward for all the sacrifices he's made and for his hard work. By contrast, Jeremy chooses to see the car differently; he feels his sacrifices and hard work have not been rewarded. The car is the same, the attitude in which it was received was completely different and it was the attitude that affected their

The Change[10]

purpose (all together now: we're here to be happy!), not the external factor at all.

If the external factor did not itself create the happy feelings in Sandip—or, indeed, the negatives in Jeremy—then these feelings must come from somewhere inside each man. Now, we can tap into our negative feelings without too much effort, but what about the good, positive feelings?

The great news is that these feelings are inside us all the time and are a boundless resource for us to tap into. Once you realize this, it's plain to see that there's no need for the external factors to make us happy! These things might be nice, but the good feelings are what we're really after.

And who doesn't want to feel good? Can you imagine choosing to feel good? I don't mean false positive thinking. I mean truly seeing the world differently.

Your computer has protection on it. What protection do you have on your life and mind?

Everything you see and hear, you have been collecting and assimilating into your own mind. Memories, news, good stuff, bad stuff, weird stuff, and the things that you never wanted to see in the first place but are now unable to 'unsee,' unable to forget. When you look for answers, you look into this stuff that has been collected. So much, and for so long.

You do have a choice, you just have to be conscious long enough to not only be aware of the choice, but long enough to actually make that choice.

There is a system that you can use to give you that choice. Broadband Consciousness helps you choose.

One reason many people feel stuck, trapped, or unhappy is that they are not living in the present moment. They are unsure of their present purpose—which we've just identified as being as simple as a happy existence—so they revisit their past and try to predict the future in their search for a solution. Little do they realize that this is the whole problem, and that by avoiding "now," they are in fact ensuring that their "now" always feels like something from which they need to escape! Eckhart Tolle goes into this in some detail in his book *The Power of Now,* in which he celebrates the gift of our wonderful Now over living in the already-written, unchangeable past or indeed the uncertain future.

The present is a delight and we should choose to enjoy it. We are at our happiest not when we are looking back to our past or forward to an imagined future, but when we are submersed in what is happening right now. The more focused on the present we are, the happier we will be. So, use your positive attitude to find the good in what you are doing and focus on it! Your purpose is to be happy; staying focused on the gifts of now, as well as using your memories in a positive way, will contribute to your happy purpose.

Every day that we are alive is a success and a gift. We live, breathe, feel, and experience; we have everything we fundamentally need to be happy. Even if we are facing challenges, we are strong and free to make those choices, fight those battles, or find peace in the acceptance of ourselves and others.

Points to remember:

Accept events as they are, in the moment

Your purpose is to be content, to grow, and to contribute

Focus on the positives and pearls in the present

Know and delight in your purpose, and the present moment

Remember who you really are

Be conscious of your choices

Know that you can choose, but are not always consciously making those choices

***

To Contact Neil:

www.neilmillard.com

neil@neilmillard.com

https://www.facebook.com/neil.millard

Nomi Bachar

Nomi Bachar is a popular keynote speaker, human potential expert, mentor, and a master at assisting people in releasing negative beliefs and habits while empowering them to draw on their inner power to focus on achievement. She is also the director of White Cedar Institute and creator of Gates of Power® Method, a revolutionary system that enhances self-development. Nomi is the author of the acclaimed book *Gates of Power: Actualize Your True Self*, a practical guide to creating the optimal self.

For over 26 years, Nomi has been lecturing and conducting life-changing workshops where she trains professionals around the globe. She has been interviewed on dozens of radio shows including CBS Radio, Voice of America, and iTunes. Her phenomenal stories of overcoming significant life challenges as well as her extraordinary successes captivate and inspire her audiences.

Ms. Bachar is dedicated to the craft of human growth and transformation. She has been the top actress, producer, and director of many popular stage productions throughout the years. She is also trained in psychodrama, Gestalt, bioenergetics, and primal therapy—all psychotherapeutic modalities that utilize expression, creativity, imagination, and intuition.

You Are The Source

Are You Walking in Your Big Shoes?

By Nomi Bachar

The truth of being the source and the creator of my life penetrated my consciousness slowly, but when it finally clicked it transformed everything…

For much of my young life, I lived dependent on other's love, protection, and validation. You could not guess that if you met the young me. What you would see is a pretty, strong-willed, talented and successful young performer who excelled in everything she put her mind to. Nevertheless, hidden from human view—including my own—inside my psyche lived a lonely sad girl caged in a sense of hopelessness.

I grew up in between wars in a country fighting for its survival, raised by two parents who escaped persecution and were struggling to provide for our bare necessities. Loving attention was not available and emotional support was nowhere to be found. As a child, the world and life seemed crushing and harsh. I felt at the mercy of it, rather than the source of it. Thus, my most meaningful lesson in life was to discover my inner power, creative talents, and my ability to manifest. And I did! I mastered the ability to pluck my heart's visions out of life's infinite possibilities and mold them, with passion and commitment, into reality.

I was born and raised in Israel, and like most young Israeli women, I served two years in the army after completing high school. I was stationed at a border kibbutz under the Golan Heights. There was beauty in the simple life in nature and in working the fields—until the war interrupted it. Then there were the long nights and the two thousand bombs that fell on that kibbutz.

When the war and the service were over, I could have used a long vacation, but the pressure to choose a career was mounting. It came as a shock to me, as well as to my parents, when I decided to audition for Bet-Tzvi, the Academy for the Performing Arts. I did not exhibit any acting talents, so my decision was puzzling. My father considered my decision very frivolous and irresponsible. He proclaimed that he did not raise me to be a gypsy, and had no intentions of supporting my studies. He expected me to enroll in the university and become a respectable scholar.

I actually expected that from myself, too, but some other voice within me was guiding me toward creative expression. That inner voice seemed to know better than I did of what I needed. Now in hindsight, it is clear to me that my enrollment into the academy started my personal journey toward reclaiming my aliveness, inner freedom, and creative expression—a journey that became my life path. I was a young woman restricted, bound, and even imprisoned by her fears, insecurities, and defensive patterns. Unknowingly, I was guided by a deep need to experience inner freedom.

In order to open ourselves to joy, pleasure, and true expression, we need to find out what holds us back and binds us. My personal journey has been one of many sheddings. Protective layers needed to melt away to first uncover despair and hopelessness. Then, it took self-awareness and self-nurturing to dissolve the fears, discover my true needs and desires, and grow beyond the pain into strength. The gift is a passionate, powerful, and creative spirit, whose company I enjoy today.

As kids, we grow up looking for love and affirmation from the outside—our parents, our teachers, our peers. We need this love like the air we breathe. In order to secure a sense of value and safety, we develop an elaborate survival structure that is supposed to attract others' attention and goodwill. Then, for the rest of our lives, we continue living with our eyes out there constantly grasping for a sense of self, a sense of power, and the symbols of success. The irony is that none of these qualities can be attained from outside. Life becomes a drawn-out effortful road of trying to feel fulfilled. No matter how much we achieve, we still feel we need more and more proof that we are valuable. What is missing is our own recognition of ourselves, our realization that we ourselves are the source of love, creativity, and power. We are, actually, already what we're looking for.

The source of life is everywhere, in everything, and it lives in us expressing as us. There is no need to look for power, love, or success outside. All of it lives within us. What we need to do is make choices, commitments, and take actions to actualize these powers. Our real and deep knowledge of this truth allows us to manifest our heart's desires and live comfortably within our own authentic being.

I believe that we are innately wired for happiness and fulfillment. The pursuit of bliss is our sacred right and our deepest yearning. We're meant to relearn how to be present in the moment and be naturally intimate with ourselves and life. We can learn to have fun and engage in pleasurable activities, as kids do. We can learn to love with abandon, likewise fools, express ourselves like the inner artist that exists in each one of us, and be as caring and responsible as a great parent. What's more, we can enjoy all of these aspects of ourselves simultaneously.

I created Gates of Power® Method and curriculum to provide people who are on the path to self-actualization with a clear roadmap and many effective tools. We all long to experience and express the best in us. We want to live with a sense of inner power, creativity and expression. We want to contribute, make a difference, and be loving and successful. The question is "how do we get there?" Here are a few tips.

TIP #1: THE FOUR GRAND QUESTIONS

When we want to get somewhere, it's wise to ask the questions that would help us get to where we're going. Asking the following questions (even if you have done so many times before) sharpens your understanding of yourself and your purpose. Take a minute to ponder these questions.

The first question: Who am I? Who are you in your essence? Not your history, your resume, your beliefs, actions, or habits. If someone would strip you from all of the above, what is the essence of you that remains?

The second question: Why am I here? What is the true meaning and purpose of your life?

The third question: What is in my way? What is presently interfering with you fully being your true, expressive self and living your purpose?

The fourth question: How do I get there? What is the inner shift that is necessary in order for you to completely align yourself with your potential and purpose?

Most people I talk to identify fear and self-doubt as what is in their way of being themselves. Yes, these do interfere. But, the compensative, defensive shell that we acquired to mask these insecurities is truly the problem. Our Defensive Self consists of habits, beliefs, energetic patterns, and behaviors that cover up our insecurities, even from ourselves. Insecurities that are concealed and unaddressed cannot be healed and strengthened. Living within the confining structure of our Defensive Self is our true blockage or cage. Self-awareness and emotional honesty help us to distinguish our truth from our cover. But, that is not enough. How do we shed the cover and become the self?

TIP #2: THE 3 ASPECTS OF THE SELF

We are all aware of different parts of ourselves. Sometimes, we are soft and vulnerable; other times, harsh and defensive. At times, we are playful and silly, and other times we are solemn, severe, and humorless.

It is natural to experience different aspects within the self. The key is to have all of the aspects work together in harmony so that we create strength and unity. Most of the time, there are conflicts between different aspects of ourselves and as a result, we feel sadness and anxiety.

When I started to observe my own inner landscape, I remember being struck by the extreme difference between my "sensitive-vulnerable" aspect and my "fierce-passionate" one. It almost felt like there were two different people living within me. When I was in my sensitive, vulnerable aspect, I could cry at the drop of a hat; while in my fierce aspect, I would experience a tremendous, relentless sense of determination. One aspect felt soft, the other somewhat hard, even harsh at times. I spent time learning to understand these seeming opposites. I realized the connection between them and found a way to unify them. You can think of aspects in terms of different energies, colors, attitudes, or ways of being inside yourself.

How are these aspects relating to each other? For example, how is the "tough guy self" relating to the "loving self," and vice versa?

How are they getting along? Is there a conflict? Which one is dominating your life?

What do you feel might be a better balance between your inner aspects?

In my own inner process and through my work with clients, I have observed three clearly defined aspects within the self. These tend to be in conflict with each other until we learn to unify them into a cohesive team under the leadership of our Expanded Self.

The Emotional Self

The Emotional Self is the aspect that contains all of our emotions. Our Emotional Self is extremely powerful and deeply affects our energy, our bodies, and our lives, even when it is repressed and shut down. It can be our gateway to ecstasy as well as to hellish suffering. Feelings are the nectar of life, and it is extremely important to clear negative feelings and move through and beyond them.

The Defensive Self

The Defensive Self is the aspect of the self that is concerned with emotional and physical survival. It originates out of the need to secure love and connection and out of fear of physical or emotional alienation. It is a "strong suit" that we create in order to feel secure and accepted. Most of us, before we engage in transformation work, live by the law of our Defensive Self at the expense of our Emotional Self. Our Defensive Self tends to criticize, confine, and penalize us. The inner war between these two aspects causes us to stay small and repressed, and when we don't feel, we cannot heal: cliché, but true.

The Expanded Self

The aspect I call the Expanded Self has different names in different traditions: the Higher Self, the Sud Guru, the Divine Spark, the Inner

Christ, Neshalma Elohit, the Observer, and so forth. What we name this aspect doesn't matter; living in its shoes does. This aspect of you is the one capable of awareness and compassionate witnessing. It possesses intuitive heartfelt knowledge and wisdom. It is capable of great courage and understanding. It knows what is genuinely "right" or "wrong" for you. It is the still voice that guides you, the healer within, the visionary, and the creative force behind your growth. It is your individual expression of the consciousness that is the Source.

This aspect of yourself is your true nature, beyond feelings that come and go, beyond your defensive construct, and your concept of yourself. It holds your essence. It aids you in the continual journey of creating and choosing what is most important to you.

The Expanded Self is the part of us that is in direct connection with Universal Wisdom. So, how come we get so stuck in our negative emotions and our defenses? The answer is we do not know how to use our Expanded Self to coach and heal the two other aspects (Emotional and Defensive). Some of my clients spend half of their life meditating. They have a very developed Expanded Self, but before they trained with me, they didn't know how to use it to transform their Defensive Self and heal their Emotional Self. Other clients have had all kinds of personal coaching and training, but, when they came to work with me, it became clear that they were still internally divided, and that interfered with them achieving fulfillment.

I created Gates of Power® Method to train people to use their Expanded Self as the inner coach and the guide it is supposed to be. When your Expanded Self is leading your life, you have true power, focus, and clarity to turn your visions into reality and be the leading force in all areas of your life.

Gates of Power® Method offers exercises and processes to help us connect to our Expanded Self and create a positive inner dialogue among all three aspects. The good news is that every one of us, without exception, is born with an Expanded Self. It is always within us. We can learn to use its wisdom to coach and transform. That takes the kind of training I offer in Gates of Power® Method.

TIP #3: THE 7 GATES OF POWER

Twenty-six years of coaching and counseling others, as well as my own personal journey, have provided me with a long, fruitful observational time. My observation revealed 7 channels or pathways of inner power through which our psyche finds expression. I call these channels "Gates." A Gate, by definition, is a portal or a doorway. Our inner being flows through these 7 Gates and expresses itself. The Gates are also portals for receiving. There is an exchange between our inner self and life. All of the Gates are interconnected and complement each other. Through them, we learn, expand, and experience life.

You can think of these Gates as 7 portals leading from and to the center of town (the center being our internal core). Over the years, as my inner work and my work with clients progressed, my knowledge and understanding of these Gates deepened. The 7 Gates of Power® are not to be confused with the chakra system, the meridians (pathways of energy in the body), or the auric layers. All these important systems of energy are acknowledged through the work with the Gates, but they are not the Gates themselves. Each Gate is a channel of experience and expression; in the Gates of Power® Method, we explore, energize, and unblock these channels. Another image that would help you understand these Gates is imagining yourself as a diamond with 7 facets. Your inner light reflects itself through the 7 facets, and the light from outside shines through, reaching your inner being.

The 7 Gates of Power® are:

1. THE GATE OF THE BODY

This Gate explores the body, its expression, energy field, and physical well-being, as well as its connectedness to our emotional and spiritual experiences. We find a way to move freely and authentically, enjoying the body's energy and physical abilities.

2. THE GATE OF EMOTIONS

This Gate reflects the power of emotions and their expression, with the aim of creating inner balance and emotional integration. We cannot be whole without the ability to experience the full spectrum of our Emotional Self. Just as a pianist needs to play all the keys of the piano, the dark and light, we need to experience our dark and light moments and find our emotional strength.

3. THE GATE OF DIALOGUE

This Gate illuminates the "inner" (within ourselves) and "outer" (with others) dialogues. The aim is to create constructive, fulfilling, and successful relationships with ourselves and others. Many of us engage in a critical and harsh dialogue with ourselves. We need to transform the inner dialogue into a positive and supportive one, so we can create strong and fulfilling relationships with others.

4. THE GATE OF CREATIVE EXPRESSION

This Gate explores and expands our ability to create and express. The aim is to use and enjoy our natural creativity in all areas of life.

5. THE GATE OF LIFE PATH

This Gate reflects personal choices, life goals, and visions. The goal is to actualize them and be a contributing force to ourselves, life, and our communities. Our life path springs from what we are most passionate about, not what we think is most logical or intellectual. Once we're clear about our heart's passion, we learn to move consistently in the right direction, making choices, commitments, and actions that take us there.

6. THE GATE OF SILENCE

This Gate explores the realm of silence, prayer, and meditation. We create a peaceful mind and develop a spiritual connection. In the silence, important questions or insights reveal themselves and a deep sense of connectedness emerges.

7. THE GATE OF KNOWLEDGE

This is the Gate of acquiring knowledge. Any knowledge (history, art, science, math, etc.) leads to the knowledge of life. Knowledge is a space of inquiry for life's big questions.

If you are committed to total well-being and fulfillment, you need to attend to all 7 facets of your life. The Gates, true to their name, are channels of inner power. They are all connected and work in synergy while each one contributes a different kind of strength to your being.

My experience shows me that most people tend to develop three or four of the Gates and neglect the other ones. That does not work in the long run. You would not think to consistently exercise only your right arm, left leg, and right shoulder if you intend to have a balanced body. The same goes for your life. A balanced and successful life means empowering and energizing all 7 Gates as a holistic unit.

You're here to be the full expression of your Expanded Self. Life's gift is our ability to experience and express our greatness and release everything that is not that. Be sure to dedicate every day of your life to creating the optimal you.

***

To Contact Nomi:

Email: nomibachar@gmail.com

Website: www.NomiSpeaks.com

www.facebook.com/gatesofpower

www.linkedin.com/in/nomibachar

www.gatesofpower.com

David Musgrave

When I first left university in the 1970s, I worked as a research scientist in agriculture for twenty years. I soon discovered that I was not like most scientists in that I was always fascinated by how the whole system worked.

Years later, one of my sons had a bad reaction to his MMR immunization at two, which developed into food allergies and very itchy eczema, which spread to most of his body.

After two and a half years of misery for him, I was given a bottle of flaxseed oil, which worked almost like magic, to heal his eczema and allergies. For me, this was a catalyst to start a twenty-five-year career studying the effects of nutrition on health.

I quickly discovered that my ability to look at my whole body as a system gave me a unique perspective and led me on my own journey to achieve wellness. Now, at **69, life is more fun** than it has ever been and I would describe myself as 99% well. Some of the knowledge that I have accumulated over the last 25 years has been condensed into this chapter to help you achieve the same results for yourself.

TAKE CHARGE of your Happiness, Belly fat, and Sexiness

A Woman's Route to Wellness

By David Musgrave

Let's see, you're feeling tired, anxious, overweight, unsexy, and often just plain cranky?

Add to that, you're totally frustrated with your weight, you've tried everything but failed, so you tried again and you failed again. This pattern really starts to do your head in and makes you feel like a failure and you just want to give up, as you start to fall into a downward spiral of low self-worth.

Maybe you've even been to your doctor and been told "I've run a few tests and they are all normal, so maybe you just need an antidepressant." If so, you're not alone; in fact, a staggering one in four women in the United States is on some form of antidepressant medication.

This scenario is very common, but is this normal? Absolutely not!

So how does it happen that we feel like this so frequently in this modern world? Unfortunately, our bodies evolved in a much simpler time, so modern living tends to push your hormones out of balance to the point that you feel like crap.

To find the answer to why this happens, we have to go back around ten thousand years to when our species lived as hunter-gatherers as we moved out of Africa to colonize the whole world. What made us so incredibly successful as a species is our amazing brain that allowed us to develop the capacity for abstract thought and communicate a wide range of emotions.

Underneath that amazing human brain is the primitive core of your limbic system, which is sometimes called the reptilian brain. Its key functions are to keep you alive and to urge you to reproduce. Our food supply in those days was often erratic, so our bodies developed some very powerful hormonal systems to make sure any excess food was stored for emergencies—as fat!

One of the key functions of your limbic system is to continuously and unrelentingly scan your environment to see whether you are "safe." If it decides you are "not safe," then it starts a hormonal cascade called the adrenalin response or very commonly the "fight or flight response."

The "fight or flight response" was first described in the 1930s by Walter Cannon and became the accepted model to describe what happens to your body when you get a fright or come under stress. So the picture has been that all the physiological changes that happen when you get stressed are designed to help you to either fight a lion, or the neighboring tribe, or if things get really sticky, be able to run away to save your life.

Now this is where things start to get really interesting for you as a woman, because most of the research that was done by psychologists to develop this model, which they called the "fight or flight response," was done on men!

When we were hunter-gatherers, the key role of men in society was to go out and kill animals for food or to defend the settlement from any attack, so it totally makes sense that in men, the primary response to stress is the fight (confront the stressor with aggression) or flight (flee from it—or in the modern world men tend to show social withdrawal or substance abuse) response.

So for men, the physiological changes that come from a surge of adrenalin to prepare them for extreme physical activity, and to minimize the damage to their body if they're wounded, are overlaid by the psychological changes that come with a surge of testosterone.

Very recently, a group of female psychologists in California realized that this model really doesn't describe the way women behave under stress at all (surprise, surprise—few men try and understand a woman's mind). So their new model, which seeks to better describe how women behave, they called "tend and befriend."

The inherent way women respond to stressful situations is to go into protective mode for themselves and their children—the "tend" part; and by seeking out a larger social group, usually women, for mutual defense (or calling your girlfriend or mother for support)—the "befriend" part. The downside of this response for women's health is that when they are stressed, women have a very strong inherent urge to look after everyone else, at the expense of looking after themselves.

It's clear from the latest research that this "tend and befriend" response has evolved in the context of women being the primary caregiver for their children and fleeing too readily at any sign of danger would actually put her children at risk.

All the adrenalin responses in women still happen, with the physiological changes that prepare you for extreme physical activity and to minimize the damage to your body if you're wounded. The key difference from men is, that instead of a surge of testosterone, for women it is overlaid by a surge of the hormone oxytocin (your cuddle hormone), which initiates the psychological behaviors that promote caregiving behavior and underlies the attachment between mothers, their children, and their 'sisters'—the "tend" part. Some studies also suggest that oxytocin enhances social contact and reduces aggression—the "befriend' part.

In long-term stress, the main hormones at work become cortisol and oxytocin, which gives you a hormone-driven way of being which can have very subtle, but highly undesirable effects on your feelings of self-worth and your feelings around your relationships.

The programmed need to tend or look after other people means that you are likely to feel that you need to take on a range of tasks, just because "I'm fine, I can do that for you," when in fact these tasks can probably be done by others without adding to your already stressful and overloaded day. This might look like you making lunches for your teenage children and partner or rushing home from work to prepare a meal for the rest of the family (when you would prefer to pop into the gym for a 20-minute workout—yes, that is all that it needs to take).

Because you are already stressed and overloaded, adding another layer of tasks to be done can add to your feelings of "I'm not good enough" because the reality is, you are not fine; you're overloaded, so you start to feel overwhelmed. You can also set yourself up for feelings of resentment against the people you are tending, which can have a very damaging effect on your relationship with them.

The other subtle effect which can happen if you take on doing tasks for your partner, which he is quite capable of doing, and probably didn't ask you to do in the first place, then you are actually treating him like a child. If you really want to kill your desire for an intimate sexual relationship with your man, then treating him like a child is a really good way to achieve this.

The Change[10]

The reality is that you're no use to anyone else if you are not well, so you have to put your own health first. If you're not dealing with your stress, then your stress hormones are giving your limbic system very subtle feelings that you need to look after everyone else first.

It's important that you realize that you are not the primitive response of your limbic system; you are so much more than that. You have the potential to modify how you respond to those subtle feelings by using your higher cortical mind and your wonderful intelligence to find a better way.

Now that you are aware of these potential subtle reactions to stress, if they are happening in your life, then you need to have the courage to talk to the others involved to find a win-win solution that works for everyone. You also need to use the techniques described later in the book to get your stress hormone levels back in balance.

Although the tend-and-befriend model does emphasize the differences between the genders, there is no suggestion that your response to stress is written in your genes. When you think about it, this really comes down to the question "who am I," because in any given situation, I am a very different person, depending on the circumstances.

So for me, who I am when I'm on the ski slopes, standing at the top of a snow half pipe, with six-meter high walls, preparing myself to ski down it, is a very different person from when I am cuddled up with my wife watching a romantic movie and the fire alarm goes off.

In the first situation, my body is in full adrenalin response, overlaid with a surge of testosterone, because I am fully in my masculine energy—but this is eustress—I am doing this deliberately for the pure joy of pitting myself against the mountain (my apologies to you women readers—you are unlikely to relate to this).

In the second situation, my body goes into distress (I didn't choose it) and the full-on adrenalin response, but this time, it is overlaid with oxytocin because we have been cuddled together and I am in my more feminine energy. So my first instinct is to make sure my wife is safe before I go to deal with whatever set the alarm off.

We can all think of how some women behave in the work environment (when they tend to be in their masculine energy), when they are under stress, they can be just as aggressive and in "fight and flight" mode as any man. Similarly, when a man is looking after his children (and is more in his feminine mode), and the children are threatened, they will also likely go into their "tend and befriend" mode to look after them.

What's important for you to realize is that while the symptoms of stress in a man can be quite different from the symptoms displayed by his partner in any given situation, underneath both your behaviors, the entire stress hormone cascade is still going on and potentially doing damage to your body.

This chapter is a lot about how the stress reaction impacts on how your body burns or stores energy (fat) and particularly, how it impacts on how your brain works and how your body responds to changes in your body chemistry—particularly your thyroid hormones and your sex hormones—in other words "your happiness, belly fat, and sexiness."

This chapter is also about how to be well.

I find it sad that when I give a talk and ask my audience to tune into their body and put a number between 1 and 100 on how well they feel, I have only once had someone put their hand up at 90 and many still haven't put their hand up at 50.

Personally, I will put my hand up for 99 and getting closer to the elusive 100. At 69 years of age, I don't do anything obsessively, but I choose my food with care (in other words I generally eat dark chocolate) and I do love butter, but saturated fats are NOT bad for you. I don't do exercise for exercise's sake, but I am very fortunate that I can easily go out and ground myself in a very beautiful piece of nature and do get a certain amount of exercise working my organic farm. I do meditate most weekdays and usually do some yoga about once a week.

In other words, I don't stress if I don't do my routine every day—because after all, it's what you do most days that determines your health and happiness, not what you do occasionally.

To me, it's important that at 69, my body doesn't limit me in any way. I will happily point my skis straight downhill for the thrill of speed or spin my wife in a fast milonga until we collapse laughing.

Trust me—getting old does not mean you have to forgo things you enjoy, or have brain fog, or be painful, or tired, or have low libido, or "Feel Like Crap" (the FLC Syndrome was first talked about by Dr. Mark Hyman—a Functional Medicine practitioner—wonderful term!). You were born to be happy here on earth NOW—not in some future realm, but you have to consciously choose to live for happiness and joy and not just let life happen to you because of your unconscious choices.

I read recently that if you have survived to reach the ripe young age of fifty, you are probably about halfway through your life. If you are roughly in this age bracket, you need to ask yourself the question "Do I want to feel the way I do now for the second half of my life?"

If the answer to this question is NO, then it's time to take charge of your own health and make some changes, probably in several areas of your life.

The reality is that studies have shown that it's much easier to prevent health problems than it is to reverse them, so the longer you leave this decision to seek wellness, the more difficult it's going to be to get to a place where your life is full of juiciness and joy—which is where we all really want to be, so I encourage you to read on.

That said, the food you eat gives your body very powerful hormonal messages—a calorie is not just a calorie and your body metabolizes and responds to carbohydrates, proteins, fats, and dietary fiber very differently. This means that for most people, a few simple changes in the areas of your life detailed below can make a major change in the way you feel within a few days.

The basic premise of this chapter is that not feeling well in any area of your life is caused by your particular combination of the three following factors—what I like to think of as the three legs of the stool of wellness, because if you neglect ANY of these three areas, your wellness stool will fall over at some point—probably when you least expect it. The three key areas are:

The Building Blocks—i.e., lack of some of the 90 odd essential nutrients. Please focus on the word essential; because lack of any of them in your diet every day means that the millions of new cells you are growing every day are less than perfect. There are also a few foods which are no no's, which you do need to avoid most of the time (note that I deliberately said avoid, not eliminate—life doesn't have be to be difficult to be fun).

Toxicity in the Body—unfortunately, our modern world is rife with chemicals produced in factories. While there are a few natural chemicals that are toxic, nearly every chemical produced in a factory is toxic to some degree, including foods. For instance, I include margarine as a toxic chemical, because there are no enzymes in nature that can digest margarine (butter is back—yeah).

In this modern world, we live in a virtual soup of synthetic chemicals, which means that unless you are actively supporting your body to detoxify on a regular basis, your own liver, bowel, kidneys, and skin detox systems are almost certainly overloaded and need your active support.

Toxicity of the Mind—when we are young, our mind acts as a virtual sponge and we believe pretty much everything that is told to us, including negative comments.

Every time you say "I can't do ….. because ….." that is almost certainly a negative self-belief which is not actually true, although your ego or left brain would like to have you think it is true. Similarly, most of us grow up with some form of the belief "I am not lovable"—which means that until you are able to let this belief go and love yourself, you are unable to fully enjoy the wonders of truly loving another person.

So your beliefs are acted out in the mind talk—the unpleasant little woman on your shoulder or your ego—which brings a lot of mental and emotional stress into your life.

How these three factors manifest in you not feeling well is totally dependent on your unique combination of these three fundamental factors. Nobody else in the world will have your unique combination.

Unfortunately, medical doctors are highly trained to fit your particular set of symptoms into a box, so they can give you a "diagnosis" and a "treatment"—usually a pill—in fact, the better doctors are at finding a "diagnosis," the more highly they are regarded by their peers.

When your body is telling you that things are just not right with it, it can be extremely comforting to get a diagnosis from your doctor—you finally know what's wrong with you—oh the relief!

The problem with a "diagnosis" is that it tells you nothing about how your particular combination of diet and toxicity of the mind and body brought you to that place. So having a diagnosis can actually get in the way of you finding what changes you need to make to get you to a state of wellness.

For instance, if you have low thyroid function, with low energy levels and you struggle with your weight, then this could have come from either:

1. Your diet being lacking in the building blocks of iodine, selenium, and iron and low in Omega-3.

To deal with this issue, you would need to start a comprehensive supplementation program, including some high-quality sea vegetables, and an Omega-3 supplement like flax seed oil and drastically cut down on the amount of carbohydrates you are eating.

2. Hashimoto's thyroiditis, which is an autoimmune condition, principally brought on by toxicity in the body.

To deal with this issue, you would need to undertake a comprehensive whole body detox program, with particular emphasis on your liver and also, in the short term, go onto a low carb, gluten-free diet to allow your gut to heal.

3. Stress brought on by your inability to say no and speak your truth in your relationships. Your ability to speak your truth is

directly related to the functioning of your throat chakra, which is why this particular stressor is most likely to impact on your thyroid.

For you to be able to actively love yourself enough to set boundaries in your relationships, you will need to deal with some issues which probably came from your childhood and start to take control of your mind. Doing some form of meditation is essential for this to work, and there are some marvelous technologies available to help with this, which allow you to get results with only 10-15 minutes per day.

You will also need to find a process that allows you to have no regrets about the past, by letting go of any resentments you hold against people in your life for real or imagined "wrongs" and find a way to forgive them.

As you can see what you need to do to correct the underlying low thyroid function completely depends on why it's malfunctioning in the first place.

Another issue can be that if some of your symptoms don't fit into the particular box your doctor wants to put you in, they are quite likely to say "it's all in your mind."

So this chapter is aimed at teaching you how to modify your three fundamental factors with the objective of helping you along the journey to wellness.

I have had it said to me "that sounds like a lot of hard work".... I don't see it that way.

For me to feel wonderful at 69 and not feel limited by my mind and body has taken a lot of knowledge. I don't see it as hard work to do the things I do—I see that my life is full of fun things to do, wonderful food to eat, and wonderful relationships.

I have written this chapter to give you the knowledge on how to do this for yourself

***

To Contact David:

Phone +64 21 355 125

Skype david.j.musgrave

http://davidmusgrave.nz/

http://wellnessdirect.co.nz/

http://waihibush.co.nz/

https://facebook.com/david.j.musgrave

https://www.facebook.com/waihibush/

https://www.linkedin.com/in/david-musgrave

Sally Kay Miller

Sally Kay Miller is a committed leadership/relationship coach that takes a stand for her clients' agendas and for the new outcomes they desire in their personal and business lives. She has a keen sense of listening, a strong toolbox of curious questions, an excellent sense of intuition, a firm understanding of leadership principles, and is extraordinarily present with her clients. Her purpose/vision is to connect courageously to each individual she works with, so that they take continuous, committed action to what they desire in their lives. She believes that when we have a dream and are taking action steps to achieving it, we get the new outcomes we desire. Her clients are enjoying stronger relationships. Sally Kay is a professional coach who has a sense of humor and throws in a dash of Hope. Her multifaceted background in business and her personal life makes her a rigorous coach who is walking the walk. She has a strong history as a speaker and trainer/teacher.

She achieved her Certification as a Professional Performance Coach and Relationship Coach from Source Point Training. She founded her own coaching business, *Raising Hope Daily.*

My Journey to Getting my HOPE back, After Losing my Child to Addiction

By Sally Kay Miller, MSA, CPPC, CRC

How do I recover and flourish again after the loss of my child? How do I go on living? These are questions I hear from my clients as a coach. This is a subject that is near and dear to my heart. My husband and I lost our son, Joe Jr., suddenly at the age of 39 almost six years ago to an overdose of cocaine. Police said it was something about how it was cut. The day Joe Jr. died was the worst day of our lives. When my husband, Joe Sr., came home early from work and said those words to me "***Joe is dead!***" I heard little after that. Unbeknownst to us, our son had been found lying dead the day before, on my birthday. He had an emergency card in his wallet that I had given the family at Christmas. Joe Sr.'s cell number was on it; that is how they knew to contact him. I felt frozen hearing those words. I could walk and talk, but everything seemed like it wasn't real—like I was in a dream state. Disbelief was my first feeling—"It can't be true"; "It must be someone else"; and "I won't let myself believe it." I knew I needed to go tell my two daughters. There were so many questions I had. Try as I might, there were no answers to the "why" questions. Why did he die? Why is this happening to us? Why do I feel it is somehow my fault? Why would God let this happen? Why, Why, Why? All I wanted to do was give up on living. My daily existence felt as if a veil of overwhelming sadness was draped over me and it was "**in place to stay**!" Yet, other times, I felt "Mad as hell." Everything from that point forward is gauged on a scale of "Before" that horrible day and "After" that day.

I will share the backstory, because although it is painful to tell, many people are living the same nightmare on a daily basis. When

Joe Jr. was a teenager, his school called to tell us their fears about Joey's future. They said Joe Jr. had the symptoms of an alcohol and drug problem and his grades had been suffering. I thought to myself, "NOT MY CHILD"! We had stayed married, went to church, were fairly good parents, and we cared. "I would know" if he had that kind of problem. He was our third child and such a sweet boy, very much wanted. I had noticed that he stayed in his room a lot listening to heavy metal music, but he was a **teenager**! He had gotten withdrawn and moody since he started 10th grade. This was much different than when he was in elementary school. His new friends were questionable and we had smelled weed on him at times. It turned out he had been skipping school to drink and get high. He came home very drunk the next week and caused a big scene with his father. Many things went through our heads. We argued and blamed each other. We had two teenage daughters, one at home (Cindy), and one on her own already (Tammy), to think about as well. Joe Sr. and I were both preoccupied; him with his cement business, me with a full-time job and working on my Master's Degree. We had been arguing a lot. I wondered if this was our fault. We decided we needed to take action.

We got our son into a six-week drug treatment center, but he ended up relapsing two weeks after he finished. They recommended a **long-term** treatment center (Alpha House), which was a one-year program that included school on campus. Our thoughts were, "No son of ours was going to be an alcoholic or a drug addict if we could help it." Boy were we in for a ride.

Joe Sr., our daughter, and I went twice a week to Joey's treatment center for the family counseling sessions. In these sessions, we got an education and met with other families that had teens there. We learned that addiction is a family disease. We were told we were all part of the problem and the solution. We learned from John Bradshaw's work that a family is like a mobile—when one part moves, it moves other parts as well. They said alcoholism/addiction is usually a multigenerational problem. That was right on, as we had alcoholism on both sides of our family, but it was not discussed much. We first believed it was solely our son's problem, but we were learning otherwise. We learned about enabling behaviors. For example: covering for him when he skipped school or taking him to school when he overslept. I thought a "Good" Mom just does those things.

It turned out that making Joey accountable for his behaviors would be very important to his chances for staying sober (they called it recovery). I read books like *Co-dependent No More* by Melanie Beatti. I took Joey a stuffed bear on our first family visit. The staff told me, "No *you* keep that." I will NEVER forget what they said next. "Mrs. Miller, would you do anything for your son, if you thought it would help him recover?" I said, "Yes of course I would. I would walk on burning coals to help my son." They said, "Then we are going to ask you to do NOTHING for your son right now." They were making him earn any "extras" he wanted. That would make him more **accountable** for his behavior.

He had daily group counseling there. We attended family group sessions with all the other families with teens there. The issues that were being discussed were rarely talked about in my generation. Such as having a "Don't talk rule" in families; (An unspoken rule to keep your mouth shut about family problems) and Getting really **honest** about everything that is going on. The treatment center recommended I join Al-Anon and I took their advice. I attended initially for Joey, but it turns out it was more for the individual attending, but did help you understand alcoholism. "All of a sudden, this is about *my* problems?" *I had a lot to learn.*

Al-Anon had some excellent slogans which were helpful tools, like "ONE DAY AT A TIME" and "LIVE AND LET LIVE." I was very overwhelmed so "One minute at a time" seemed like all I could handle. Another important slogan was, "YOU DIDN'T CAUSE IT AND YOU CAN'T CURE IT!" I was glad to find out I didn't cause it at least. You didn't have to talk at Al-Anon, but I was on a mission to help myself and my son. I got honest about my current family and my family of origin. I now had my own program of recovery.

Joe Jr. graduated from Alpha House after being there for a year. Our whole family was elated that he had completed the program. We were all healthier as a family with all our new knowledge. We had a sober, happy, more humble son back and our daughters had their brother back. He attended Alcoholics Anonymous (AA) and Narcotics Anonymous (NA), which helped him stay on program. He was now being accountable for his own behavior. I let him run his program of recovery and I led mine. He stayed sober and graduated high school. Later, he met a wonderful woman and married her. It was a day we will never forget, a lovely wedding merging two beautiful young people. We loved his wife and her family. He continued to work in our family cement business. He had a baby girl. They were such wonderful years for our whole family. Every day I thanked God for Joe Jr.'s sobriety. This went on for fifteen years.

Then, Joe Jr. **relapsed**. For six stressful years, we were on a roller coaster ride with him. He ended up getting a divorce from a woman and a family he dearly loved and eventually he lost everything he had held dear. Joe Sr. and I sent him to three more treatment centers, one for a year (Narconon). He just couldn't seem to get back on track. Our beautiful son ended up dead. The son we welcomed into this world as a product of our love. His father's namesake was now GONE. He was found in a hot apartment after laying dead for several days. He was so decomposed we weren't allowed to see his body. Forensics had to use dental records to identify him.

After his death, I lost my hope. Joe Sr. was even worse than me, crying all the time. I needed something. I cried, sobbed, and screamed when I was alone. I felt I had to hide my feelings and "Put

The Change[10]

on a good face." My moods were unpredictable. Despite that, I courageously read a letter to my son at the funeral, without crying. Later, I felt like I had fallen in a pit of sorrow. There are several **stages** of grief—denial, anger, bargaining, depression, and acceptance, not always in that order. I was experiencing many of these. I'm sure all of you that have lost a child understand the agony I felt. It really doesn't matter the cause of the death or the age of the child. Our children are not supposed to die before us.

I went on like that month after month for a year. I will never forget the day my Granddaughter Autumn, (daughter of Cindy), visited us at our Florida home. There had been a large miscommunication in our family that day. Cindy, Chris (her husband), and Haleigh (her other daughter) were here visiting us. Autumn sat the entire family down and discussed a series of meetings she had recently gone through. She told us how they had changed her life and were monumental for her. She invited us to consider attending these transformational workshops. She knew it would help enhance our communication as a family. We had all suffered so much since Joe Jr. died.

I was so hungry for anything that might bring me out of my grieving and sadness. I was definitely willing to try anything to help me "help myself." I went to The Discovery, Breakthrough, and The Leadership Program in New York City, New York, directed by Michelle Gesky. This set of workshop experiences is meant to be an **interruption** in a person's thinking. It was life changing for me. While I am not at liberty to discuss the methods, I can share some insights I gleaned from the experience. One discovery was that I was operating from a "victim mentality" which wasn't allowing me to access my happiness or power. I felt I had EVERY right to feel like a victim, after everything I had been through. It was like a literal slap in the face or wakeup call. I can thank Lou Dozier, co-owner of Source Point Training, for that. I NEVER came so close to belting someone in my life as I did that day. As it turns out, though, she was the catalyst/interruption in what I call my mouse in a cage, circular destructive thinking. I was always doing the same things, leading to the same bad outcomes. I *chose* to go outside my comfort zone to take on my life in a whole new way after that awakening. I was a "human doing, not a human being." In other words, I did many things daily, met many goals, but I had no passion and felt no **Joy.** I received a "New toolbox" available to me now, especially in relationships and my new way of "being." Don't get me wrong; I was still very sad, but I had decided to take action and live for myself and my son Joe Jr. I identified that my true passion was to work with people like myself who had suffered large monumental losses. I first needed to grieve and heal in order to "clean up" my own demons. I felt like I was waking up to life *without* losing my connection to Joe Jr. in my heart. All of the tools I gained helped my relationships with both of my daughters.

Grief is like a millstone around one's neck, or a heavy burden. Grieving feels at times like being in limbo; "an uncertain situation that you feel you cannot control and in which there is no progress." You might say you feel "stuck" there. There are tools that helped me while grieving that may be helpful to you to get your hope back. The number one thing was *"To give myself permission to live again."* It takes a *conscious decision*, being *present* in the current moment, and taking *action* to break out of that melancholy, unhappy state of mind. Some say getting unstuck is either hard or it is easy, and either way they will be correct. It takes *accountability* for your actions. You always have an opportunity to create your own story or script. So what if you say it is easy! As strange as it sounds, it can work. Al-Anon says, "Fake it 'till you make it." Changing any habit takes commitment and believing in one's self. What you will be doing is reprogramming your brain to think differently. At first it may be for a few minutes, then more and more time, and you are on your way.

The Change[10]

Another tool is *"Giving up the story you are telling yourself"* that is keeping you in a victim mode. You have the right to the story and to what occurred. However, by staying in your feelings, you *choose* to have no *power* over the story. My "Aha" moment was at a meeting. Yours can be at this very moment. Is there something you would like to do in honor of your child, if you set your grief aside, but not your love? Then get in action to do it, whatever it takes. You can start with one thing. There are no small steps and each step is a step toward hope.

It is so true that the loss of a child can "Make or break a marriage." I decided to start by working on my deteriorating relationship with my husband. He was so grief stricken that he cried daily, and had lost his passion for life. I was determined to reconnect with Joe Sr. in an authentic, loving way that would even surpass what we had prior to our loss. I made a *commitment* to rekindle and strengthen our relationship for the next four months. I had learned about a tool called "Creating an Intention." The dictionary defines *intention* as: a thing intended, an aim or plan. My intention was to do two things daily—1. To be with my husband in an authentic, positive, and loving way; 2. To ask God daily to put something right in front of me; if he had a **purpose** for me, I would no longer search for anything.

A dear friend, who had also attended all three transformation workshops, asked me to listen in on a conference call about becoming a **Life Coach**. I agreed to listen. I declined to do it, due to my daily intentions. Several days later, I was fishing on our boat with Joe Sr. out in Charlotte Harbor, when I noticed it was very cloudy. My phone rang and it was Barbara Fagan, co-owner of Source Point Training, following up on the conference call. She asked me one simple question, "Sally Kay, have you ever felt that you fulfilled your *purpose* here on earth?"

"I STOPPED DEAD IN MY TRACKS. AT THAT VERY MOMENT, THE CLOUDS SEPARATED AND A STREAM OF LIGHT CAME DOWN TO THE WATER FROM HEAVEN."

I asked her to wait a minute while I took a picture of what I was seeing. Then I looked beside me and a dragonfly (our group mascot for my three-part transformational journey) landed on our boat right next to me. Then it hit me—I was destined to do **this in Honor of my son**. I would live for BOTH of us from this moment on. This was the answer of my second intention "PUT IT RIGHT IN FRONT OF ME AND I WILL DO IT." I returned to the phone and said, "Barbara I am in! No matter what it takes, I am supposed to do this." I had no idea how I could afford it, but I believed, with no evidence, that I would do it. The universe/God was picking me. I also heard a little voice in my head saying, "Sally Kay, just go for it. It will all fall into place." Now, here I am, writing this about my awesome journey. I became a Certified Professional Performance Coach and Certified Relationship Coach. I dedicated my business (*Raising Hope Daily*) to Joe Jr. I stand for others in his memory. I have a purpose, a mission, and my Hope back.

I now coach women who have suffered due to a catastrophic loss, such as the loss of a child, a job, a divorce, or problems in any of their relationships.

I am a believer in signs. When we are present, open, and willing to see with new eyes, we are shown more than we ever imagined. Ten minutes ago, while writing, I saw a dragonfly **land on the wall inside my house,** giving me a sign that I am right on track sharing this story. There is Hope and my son and I are "Raising" it every day. When you live with purpose, taking action steps, you realize your dreams can become your reality, and you can have your Hope back.

***

To Contact Sally:

www.raisinghopedaily.com

www.facebook/RaisingHopeDaily

Phone: 810 434 0632

Terry Nadine Taylor

Terry Taylor is **passionate** about people wanting to make a difference in the world. Terry's coaching **promise** is Clarity, Alignment, and Action. Her **Purpose** is to courageously explore values and barriers to increase potential and manifest a peaceful and cohesive future. Terry's **Values** are challenge, contribution, passion, integrity, initiative, love, independence, humor, and zest. She is committed to manifesting her **Vision**, including beautiful surroundings, joy-filled memories, radiant smiles, and peaceful communications.

As an executive coach, Terry Taylor works extensively in leadership development, organizational change, and lean process improvement. Since 1991, Terry has provided over 5,000 hours of executive leadership and team coaching. She coaches to engage teams to build a better business and deliver higher value to customers. She has helped over a thousand people throughout the United States and internationally to deepen learning and implement change.

Terry holds a Masters in Organizational Psychology from Antioch, earned the Master Coach designation from the International Coach Federation, and completed the University of Washington Lean Six Sigma Black Belt certification program. Terry's background provides a comprehensive, in-depth platform for change mastery. Her clients are leaders and executives in hospitals, financial institutions, physicians groups, not-for-profit organizations, and businesses across many industries.

Liberate the Leader in You

By Terry Nadine Taylor

It takes energy and focused intention to be the leader and create the life you want. It doesn't happen on its own. It isn't reserved for lucky people. Neither your parents, nor Mr. or Mrs. Wonderful can provide it. It is up to you to create and it will proceed from you when you take the helm.

And, know in advance that having a dream takes courage. And, that it takes persistence to visualize it. Taking steps, large and small, requires fortitude. And, even though you'll be planning, let go of the need to know how to implement it. It takes wisdom to let your plans unfold. Take charge of the assets you have: Time, Money, and Energy.

If you're curious about where your priorities lie, take a look at your calendar and checkbook. Where you spend your time, money, and energy reveals what you truly prioritize.

This sounds so absolute, and it is. Steve, in his twenties and on the verge of life's beginnings, was permanently injured in a brutal car accident. Enduring years of physical therapy, multiple surgeries, and searing disappointments over his lost abilities, he could have chosen to resent this twisted fate. He didn't. He retook the helm and chose to direct his life and meet the challenges.

Happiness is the feeling of authorship of and contentment with life. This statement takes a moment to digest. I'm not saying accident victims are responsible for their injuries or that there aren't justified victims of birth defects, crimes, or acts of nature. I am saying accident victims are responsible for their response to the choices leading up to that moment, putting themselves in the circumstances where an accident could occur.

It's not Steve's fault. This is not a discussion of fault or blame; it is about how he chose to feel authorship and power over his life. Our society condones Steve feeling mad, sad, and resentful. But Steve chose to accept what is true and take ownership of his attitude, relationships, and physical well-being. Taking ownership of our choices and results requires **accountability**.

Personal accountability is an idea, not a pillory. It's an attitude that empowers us to take charge and change our circumstances.
Need more feedback than your calendar and bank statements? Get a gauge on reality so you can take charge. Ask the people who spend time with you what they observe about your priorities. Note your own mental chatter. Attune to the messages you are getting from your body. This inquiry is easiest with compassion for yourself. Let go of the shoulds, coulds, and woulds and take a look at your relationship with yourself. If Me with Me isn't working, nothing else works.

Mary was sick of her hour-long commute. She wanted to escape the freeway as fast as possible, and always arrived at work angry. After converting her felt experience to feedback, and examining her choices, she was able to come to a conclusion that improved her daily attitude. What did she do? She set cruise control at one mile an hour under the speed limit.

Mary's image of herself is that she is powerful. Power on the freeway manifested as anger. The anger came because her desired image of self didn't align with reality. At first, the suggestion to stop speeding seemed silly to her, but her powerful choice to participate in the commute differently changed her life energy.

We project an image to gain acceptance—starting with acceptance of ourselves. We establish a comfort zone and judge ourselves by our intentions. That's where guilt comes from; wishing we were some other way.

We then seek the acceptance of others. Because our brains are wired for connection, we desire relationships. But fear of judgment affects our ability to be open. We are afraid of losing, hurting someone, or becoming vulnerable. So we hide, defend, pretend.

We present a mask of invulnerability, competence, nicey-nice person, or winner. Turns out we interpret these masks as insecure, know-it-all, weak, or brinkman. Either way, these masks are the source of suffering—as we hide our true selves in an attempt to gain approval.

People sense a fake image, and it seeds stories about disingenuous connection. What they make up <u>could</u> be about us, and it is definitely about themselves. Alongside this outward facing image is the truth we know about our authentic selves—and we must gain the courage to discover and present this truth.

Do the work to free yourself, rather than remain leashed to someone else's opinion of you. The greater congruency between your image and the truth about yourself, the more integrity you will have in both your own eyes and the eyes of others. Choosing your approach to change and growth is the fundamental decision that defines your life experience. Here are the primary approaches people choose when addressing personal change. Which response best illustrates you?

1. **Rebel:** You can't make me! Who do you think you are?

2. **Withdraw:** Maybe I can remain safe if I sink into the wallpaper and no one will notice!

3. **Emulate:** There's a successful looking person, I'll do that!

4. **Take charge:** If it is to be, it is up to me.

Clearly, choices 1-3 are defensive approaches that keep you from having to take responsibility. Take charge and begin the work without delay.

Take the shortest route to personal accountability: personal honesty and response-ability. Assess your willingness to accept your circumstances and your ability to respond. If you find yourself in your stuck behaviors, reach out to others to get the support you need. This is the defining moment in which you take responsibility for your outcomes.

Asking for and accepting support can seem antithetical to the powerful image you might hold of yourself. Recognize this work isn't easy, and no one has the ability to objectively evaluate themselves. You want to break the habit of looking outside yourself to ensure safety.

Yet, every successful person will attribute some portion of their success to the power of the support they receive from others.

It's easier to let someone else do it for us or hold someone else responsible for our happiness. We secretly hold on to knowing we're right, and when our elected Responsible Person disappoints, we resent them. Rather than grab hold of the responsibility, we spend our energy being critical and resentful.

Is it possible to flip the switch? Yes. You can stop giving others the power to make decisions for you, and decide to make those decisions on your own. And guess what – that's what everyone actually wants in the first place. It's your life—own it.

To know what decisions to make, remain true to what you believe in. The foundational principles that you hold on to will guide you to a life of fulfillment.

Start by asking leading questions: Who am I? What are my values? What is my purpose? The answers to these, though intangible, will be your guiding star. While your vision and goals change as you progress through life, your values and purpose never change—and define who you are.

Values are the experiences that make you come alive. Some of these values are so important to us that we will chew glass to experience them. They are beacons that help you make choices leading to the most satisfied life. It's estimated that there are over 350 value words—and each of us has a unique subset. These are what drive us.

To discover what values matter to you:

- Take time to tap into yourself to recall and reflect.

- Make note of positive and negative memories and record the feelings. Only include experiences that have an impact on your sense of well-being (internal experience) and not those that necessarily resulted in praise (external affirmation). Remember that your values stem from your needs—consisting of things such as Physical well-being, Autonomy, Peace, Meaning, Play, and Connection.

- Write an initial list that bridges your personal experiences with your cultural values—as well as the universal human needs defined by our biological makeup. The wording should hold strong personal resonance for you.

- Narrow down the list by identifying the words that describe your driving needs and separate them from the strategies you use. Example: a value is "make a difference," a strategy is "contribution."

- Write about how you live these values to gain greater clarity about how you make meaning.

Purpose, meanwhile, is the alignment of passion, profession, vocation, and mission. To define your purpose, ask these questions:

- What is it that you love to do and for which you have talents? The answer is your **passion**.

- What is it that you are good at and can be paid for? The answer is the right **profession.**

- What is it I have and others are willing to pay for? The answer is **vocation.**

- What is it that I have and the world needs? The answer is **mission**.

Now that you have your values and purpose established, you're ready to move on to envision the life you want—and what it will take to get there.

Vision is the road map of life. You can base it on what you lack now, or on the life you imagine. It consists of using logic and planning to achieve your dreams, hopes, and aspirations. Your vision should resonate with your values to generate energy and enthusiasm.

Give yourself permission to dream and let go of the expectations others have for you. Blast out a long list of dreams, wishes, hopes, and desires. For some people, this might be a list of five dreams. For others, it could be a list of 30, 50, or more. Imagine your life if these dreams come true. Visually display or write a one-page description of what this looks like.

- What would there be more of?

- What secrets would you be sharing?

- What would you have accomplished?

- What legacy would you leave behind, and for whom?

- Make this exercise fun. You may want to set your answers aside for a while and come back to add more magnetism, more vivacity.

- How will you feel about yourself?

- What kind of people are in your life? How do you feel about them?

- Where do you live? Think specifics.

- What are you doing?

- What's your state of mind? Happy or sad; content or frustrated?

- What does your physical body look like? How do you feel about that?

- Does your best life make you smile and make your heart sing? If it doesn't, dig deeper and dream bigger. Stay focused on the results and plan on updating this vision statement on a regular basis.

Once you've defined your vision for the future, take stock of your life as it currently is and compare it to your vision and values.

Draw a circle and make a pie chart. Label the wedges with the areas of your ideal life. Include areas that are working well, ones you'd like to add, and those you want to improve. Rank each wedge based on how satisfied you are with that area. Use a scale of 1-10, 10 being the outside edge of the circle and 1 being the center of the circle. How balanced do the wedges look? If it were a wheel, would you make it down the road?

As you assess your current state, leave judgment aside. Instead, ask yourself, "Am I willing to pay the price to create the life I want? What is this price?"

Your answers, become the "why" and the "how." How you spend your time, money, and energy are the strategies to get there.

Start with a reality check around **energy**. Use a scale of 1 to 10 to rate your level of satisfaction for the following questions:

- What is the quality of your life energy? Is it filled with negativity or is it positively energetic?

- Are you involved in, and contributing to, positive relationships?

- Do you have a sense of purpose and are you happy with how you are pursuing it?

- How do you gauge your relationship to yourself and your health?

- How do you engage in life?

- Does your physical space support your well-being? Is your house, wallet, and car clean and orderly?

- Are your clothes, appliances, equipment in good repair?

- Are you spending energy tolerating unhealthy relationships or unworkable or undesirable circumstances?

Next analyze your **money**. Money fuels our passions. It is not the source of our passion, but it helps you get there. It is a tangible expression of your passion and creativity. Money is a way to discover what you truly value—and to measure the value that others place on your contributions.

It's now time to rate your current level of satisfaction regarding money on a scale of 1-10:

- What is the difference between your current income and expenses?

- How secure are your sources of income? If you lost one job, project, or client, would it put you in a tough situation?

- How close are you to paying off your debt?

- How much money do you have available for new ventures or emergencies?

- Do you have regular conversations with people who can help you grow your understanding of money?

- How much money do you need to be satisfied?

Finally, take control of your **time**. Locate a time blocking tool online. A time blocker is a simple 8 column table. The first column consists of your waking hours and the following seven are filled with the days of the week.

Develop daily routines. Choose a timeframe—whether a week or a month—and project how you want to spend your time. Use color pencils to differentiate activities. Recognize that many tasks take longer than you first expect. Continually evaluate and improve your daily routines. But most importantly, commit to sticking to your experiment! After you have time planned out on the blocker, make copies for each week you are testing. Write actual activities over the colored blocks and evaluate, learn, and streamline your routine.

Every morning, while you're planning, identify the 3 hardest things you HAVE to get done that day, block them in and do them. Bring these tasks in line with your values through prayer, meditation, or a personal proclamation.

Be the captain of your life by maintaining the routine of handling what's most important, seeking support, casting your vision for success, and affirming yourself. Personal mastery is the ability to maintain a clear vision of where you are heading, simultaneous with a clear assessment of where you are.

It is a discipline of continually clarifying and deepening your personal vision, of focusing your energies, of developing patience, and of seeing reality objectively. You master your results by becoming clear about which values drive your behavior and decisions to fulfill your purpose.

When we set up our lives consciously to have the preferred experience of our values more of the time, we are on the path of creating a joyful life. Clarity about life's purpose and values and implementing strategies about how to use your time, money, and energy lead you to achieve goals that move you closer to the vision you have for your life.

S.M.A.R.T. people create goals to attain their vision. Goals that are Specific, Measurable, Attainable, Relevant, and Time-based. So let's say your vision is of yourself receiving an award for a scientific breakthrough and you are accompanied by family who love and admire you. Your vision includes your friends joining you afterwards for a celebration at your beautiful home on the river.

Work your way back from the end goal to the first step. During the process, ask yourself the following questions:

- What beliefs would you have needed to change?

- What habits or behaviors would you have had to cultivate or eliminate?

- What type of support would you have had to enlist?

- How long will it have taken you to realize your best life?

- What's the most important choice you would've had to make?

- What would you have needed to learn along the way?

Write your goals S.M.A.R.T. Follow it with an objective statement and anchor the activities to your values. Example:

Goal: A well planned party for 30 people which takes place September 30, 2037.

Objective: Celebration

Value: Honor

The process of developing your vision statement is iterative—as each goal you achieve changes the work and the horizon. So revisit and rework your vision statement as part of your routine—remaining mindful of your values and what needs to happen to make each goal a reality. Ask yourself the best ways to spend your time, money, and energy. Get support from friends, family, professionals—and stay the course.

Why doesn't everybody do this? Intentional change is intimidating to many—as it takes people to the edge of their comfort zone. Just ask any dieter or soon-to-be ex-smoker. Because of this, without ongoing intervention, many people slip back into their old way of doing things. It's easier to remain with what we know, even if it's painful, then to put in the effort necessary for successful change. However, once you align your reality with your values and your vision, change becomes not only possible, but unstoppable.

We can't change when we have competing or misaligned values. We need to dig deep to learn what will help us achieve our goals. Then we must evaluate the competing priorities and commitments that take away from our focus.

Your dream life is yours to create—limited by nothing but your ability to imagine. So Liberate the Leader in You. Define your values and vision, then align your decisions and routines so you focus your actions on what you want. Use your time, money, and energy strategically—and set S.M.A.R.T. goals that align with your purpose. Your purpose and vision create the magnetic draw to pull you across the zone of discomfort and into the field of joy you imagined on the other side. You are the leader! Your vision becomes reality!

***

To Contact Terry:

www.VersoriaOnline.com

Terry@VersoriaOnline.com

360-789-3711

Michelle Gesky

Michelle Gesky has 20 years of experience in consulting, training, executive and personal coaching and development, as well as business operations. She is a Certified Relationship, Leadership, Health, and Wellness Coach, Speaker, and Author. Michelle is an intuitive and compassionate powerful coach, committed to generating that her clients live authentic, purpose-filled joyful lives full of possibility.

Michelle held senior positions at Franklin Covey as Senior Client Partner, and at Judlau Contracting as Manager of HR/Training and Development. She was Vice President of Strategic Relationships at Global Performance Solutions for many years before being hired as General Manager at Launch, a NYC post-production house in Advertising. Previously, she was in the Investment Banking Division at Goldman Sachs in HR/Leadership Development and Training, working with the Managing Directors and experienced hires. Consulting assignments included Fortune 500 Corporations and small and mid-sized companies in a wide range of industries. After years dedicated to business professionals in the corporate arena, she is now living her passion by empowering her clients to dig deep, get curious, and shine brightly with exuberance, freedom, and power in their own lives. She loves to kayak, paddleboard, travel, and spend time with her three children and her dogs.

The "Sh#*%" Word

By Michelle Gesky

Have you ever noticed that there are some things we just don't talk about? In fact, there are things we don't like to even think about. Those things have the power to plummet us into deep, yucky feelings and thoughts, which include, guilt, fear, hopelessness, lack of worth, and experiencing ourselves as not good enough, defective, different, alone.

I have coached thousands of clients over time and one thing that screams to be discussed, but which gives people the Heebie-Jeebies, is anything that causes us to experience the S word: Shame. We don't like to hear the word repeated, right? It makes us uncomfortable to think about someone else feeling the S word! Uh oh, and what about ourselves.?!!!. We'd almost rather chew on glass. You may be thinking about skipping this chapter right about now, just so you don't have to read further, right? "I'll deal with it later," we often think to ourselves. "I don't have time for *this*" (this being an opportunity to get into closer relationship with your very own personal shame) ... Maybe you're thinking that you don't have a problem with it… hmmm could be... But it could also be that you don't give yourself permission to acknowledge that more than likely shame lives within you, awakening when you are in the throe of an unhealthy dynamic. Like the monster under our bed as children that we were so scared of, we fear and dread shame. When I was a child, we were told not to say the world "Hell," as if saying it would bring the devil, horns and all, to pop up wherever we were. My clients have always resisted discussing shame, or any topic which triggers shame as we work together. Shame is, to use an analogy, the devil in the room with us.

Shame is a five-letter word, but we have more fear about speaking about shame then we have of saying that four-letter word we are all so familiar with. I can relate and through much of my life, I have tried to avoid shame at all costs, until I learned that shame is hardwired into us as a benefit, to help us survive as human beings. Shame can be a game changer.

Shame as benefit

Shame, it turns out, is hardwired into our collective DNA, probably to keep us functioning as a society, tribe, or family. Shame goes back to our primordial days, perhaps when we survived by staying together against the elements—Dinosaurs? Harsh weather? Hard to find food or water? It was a basic survival lifestyle. Shame allows us to query ourselves, to correct, redirect, and re-member ourselves with the people around us. Shame helps us to say "Is what I have done or not done, said or not said, something that I need to examine?" "Where am I misaligned with my values, my integrity, or the integrity of the group I'm in?" Shame helps to acknowledge something could have been handled differently. In our Dinosaur days, being able to access shame would have perhaps allowed someone to stay in a group, to survive rather than be kicked out into the wild, alone to face potential death. In that way, shame is healthy for us all. It is a definite diagnostic tool we can use. We must re-learn how to address shame when we are suddenly in the midst of it so that we are able to use it to move us forward instead of keeping us stuck where we are.

In my chapter on shame in *Authentic Alignment, Wise Women Reveal the Secrets of a Stellar Life,* I posit that shame is analogous to an indicator light in your human programming system that shows something is awry within the heart of you. The operating system runs quietly in the background, but sometimes programs need to be updated. As an adult, you have the choice to use the new updated system (in this case, healthy shame) or the old one installed by your parents and society (unhealthy shame). The authentically aligned you is using the uncomfortable experience of shame to communicate with you. The heart of you is your authentic self, your center which steers you and is made up of your values, beliefs, assumptions, and our true north, which some may call soul. When something occurs—and it could be an outside event, action, dialogue, or an internal self-dialogue that starts because we are judging ourselves—then we may be pulled away from our center and into what I'll call the old shame drama which distorts your perception of yourself and your situation. This is where shame takes center stage and ultimately steals the show.

> *"We don't see things the way they are; we see them the way we are."* -The Talmud

Shame has two guises, healthy and unhealthy. The shame I described above with the Dinosaur lifestyle is the healthy shame, a little uncomfortable, but powerfully re-directive if we know how to read it. When my clients learn to be deeply curious about shame's message, make different choices, and learn from what it communicates, healthy shame is a wakeup call. If not, the unhealthy shame is an undertow pulling you out of yourself, away from your center, underneath the water where we experience the sensation of drowning in our emotions. The emotions are from our core beliefs, assumptions, assessments, and thoughts. Symptoms of unhealthy shame are the icky feelings: unworthiness, avoidance, humiliation, self-loathing, anger, sadness, fear of being abandoned, looking bad, being wrong, being confronted, or found out. You may even perceive yourself as the mistake, rather than understanding, *"I made a mistake, but I am not the mistake."* Knowing this is the critical path to freedom from unhealthy shame. The reality is, if you can look below the surface to your own internal self-mechanisms, you can change your relationship with shame from unhealthy to healthy.

Our Interpretations create our Shame

Our relationship with ourselves is based on many things, but with shame, the most important is our relationship to our thoughts. Our thoughts are based on our interpretation of things and what we have learned to be true. This comes from childhood. These thoughts and core beliefs impact how we make choices in our lives today. Let's look at how it works.

Imagine if when you were very young, you saw a dog coming toward you. Suddenly, that dog got hurt. You might make a connection that when a dog comes toward you, it gets hurt.

Therefore, you start to avoid dogs, not wanting to hurt them. The truth is that the dog getting hurt had nothing to do with you. This kind of collapse between two separate events into one and your inability at a young age to use logic creates an incorrect assumption. That assumption turns into a belief that you cause dogs to get hurt, and that influences your assumption about what to do the next time you are faced with a dog. All this may occur beneath your conscious thoughts; therefore, you do not necessarily recognize that these early childhood beliefs are part of <u>your always</u> having the feeling that you should avoid dogs! This creates a conscious choice to step across the street, though you don't remember the reason why. Now as an adult, you are wary of dogs!!! To sum up, in that example and in life, our beliefs and assumptions are often driven by thoughts or beliefs that may not be the truth. Our own beliefs, coming from the past, often drive our shame and so must be observed!

Integrating "our thoughts create our reality" into your awareness moving forward is vital to freeing yourself from shame's grip. Once you can look at your thoughts and beliefs to see what is activating your shame and the emotions around shame, you can start to let go of the unhealthy shame energy.

The Anatomy of Unhealthy Shame

Some of the thoughts that encompass your experience of shame come from what you learn as a child from your parents, your church, synagogue, mosque, schools, society, etc. It's inauthentic because they are not your true beliefs, but inherited. As a child, you held people's repeated judgments as truths, rules, and regulations that governed you. Remember at the beginning of this chapter I mentioned that we are hardwired to feel shame to keep us as part of the pack? The reason we will experience these internal thoughts, judgments, and feelings is that we remember them from our youth as the voice of adulthood, telling us how to correct our actions/inactions so that we could stay safe. Therefore, we would not get separated from the pack. We experience the voice of shame as a parental figure that we needed to trust. The messaging is unhealthy and painful, but we feel it is there to protect us/love us. It is there to ensure that we are accepted by our parents and others. We therefore struggle as conscious adults to uncouple ourselves from our historical, outdated voice of shame. Uncoupling ourselves from shame makes the inner child within the adult feel out of control and abandoned.

Most of us recognize unhealthy shame. We abhor the feeling and yet we feel it so frequently we are almost unconscious of it. When you look in the mirror, what do you say to yourself? What is the inner voice? Is it judgmental or critical, or is it telling you "hey, you are really beautiful/handsome today?" When we look in the mirror, we are often not simply looking at ourselves, but we are hearing the voice of shame (other people's potential criticisms and judgments). Often we have rapid, fleeting thoughts almost at the speed of sound.

The only way that we actually know that they are shame-based thoughts is that suddenly we feel mad at ourselves, have a moment of self-loathing, sadness, or feeling of alienation before we stuff it down. The thought happened so fast that we only mostly unconsciously recognized what it was saying. How many times have you walked by someone and you perceived them as silently judging you? In that uncomfortable moment, shame is taking the stage. You walk by them on the street, for example, and never see them again. However, the shame is vocal now and you can feel its presence in your demeanor, attitude, and perhaps even in its being experienced as a lack of self-worth, or through your anger.

Take a moment now to stop reading after this paragraph and start to ask the following questions. Doing so is a courageous act that will support you, bring you clarity, and create positive steps toward a healthier relationship with yourself. When was the last time I felt shame? What does shame feel like to me? How often do I feel shame? Do I recognize my experience of shame for what it is or do I just judge myself and get angry at myself?

What is the worst part about my personal shame? How does it affect me? What are the behaviors I exhibit when I feel shame? What would I like to change in my relationship to my shame?

What did you take away about your relationship to shame? Can you tell if your shame is from your own internalized, but slightly awry thoughts and beliefs or is it the shame from younger days when you listened to the world around you for cues as to how to behave?

An example of how shame can affect you can be seen by taking a peek at an example from my own life.

When I was young, my mother took me to a modeling assignment. I told my mom I felt ill. She thought it was nerves. I vividly

The Change[10]

remember to this day the experience of climbing on these big white cubes to stand on for the photo shoot with the bright lights on us, the darkness all around, and the photographer saying, "Honey, why are you so slow? You are the youngest, yet you are moving like a sloth." What's a sloth?? I only knew I felt like I was about to throw up. I said, "I don't feel well," but the photographer and my mother ignored me. I threw up all over the cubes and on some of the assistants. I could feel the other models looking at me and I felt alone, outcast, and criticized by the photographer. I felt shame. I wanted to belong so badly; I didn't want to do the wrong thing ... Why did I experience shame? In this instance, I had outside help from the photographer and the other models' judgments. But I also internalized it and judged myself unequal. Remember, our shame is personal and from our culture around us, like our families. My shame came from my parents always trying to avoid shame themselves. My dad was an attorney in a big old, white-shoe, Wall Street law firm. My dad started out poor, a foreigner, without connections. He felt he had to fit in, to make it there. My mom went from the city to the suburbs to raise me. She was a working woman. The ladies in the suburbs didn't work and mom tried hard to act and participate in the same ways the suburban women did. That was the strong subconscious message I had from my parents. Survival means looking good and fitting in, following the rules. You can see why I had shame at that age. My parents were already modeling looking good, fitting in, and not breaking the rules and communicating it to me verbally and non-verbally. I felt I didn't fit in, look good, and wasn't following orders. My own internal sense of shame became activated. Except, remember, it really came from my parents' need to avoid shame. It didn't originate from me, but it was within me.

So let me tell you how shame shows up now as an adult. Unhealthy shame appears as an indicator that I am acting outside the lines of my comfort zone and it doesn't feel good. My tendency is to hide.

Instead, I can choose quickly to rewire how I process that shame, choose not to listen to the old shame system, but instead check in with my internal thoughts. I can learn what's really going on for me. I am gentle with myself looking for what I can do to move me forward in a shame-free direction by taking immediate action. We are wired to feel shame. This is a benefit if you can uncoil the thoughts that don't serve you, and the beliefs that are no longer relevant or true about who you are today. Our bodies are also designed to help us, in that our brain's internal limbic system, which is the brain's emotional dashboard, can help us. A scientist named Dr. Mathew Leiberman discovered that using simple language to name our emotions actually quiets the arousal in our limbic system. So, talking about shame with someone trusted helps us quiet the emotional pain.

You are strong and resilient (hey you are still here, right?), you are multitasking in a busy modern world with many distractions. You are a good person who has made mistakes just like the rest of us. In essence, part of our beauty is in our humility that we are not above or below others, that as human beings we make mistakes. Healthy shame helps us acknowledge that we all make mistakes and are hopefully learning from them. Healthy shame is there to guide as like a GPS to auto correct ourselves. Healthy shame is meant to keep us in integrity with who we say we are and who we want to be.

"Your time is limited, so don't waste it living someone else's life. Don't be trapped by dogma-which is living with the results of other people's thinking. Don't let the noise of others' opinions drown out your own inner voice. And most important, have the courage to follow your heart and intuition."- Steve Jobs, Co-founder, Chairman, CEO of Apple Inc.

The Change[10]

Tools for transforming your relationship to shame

Start a gratitude journal. Center yourself for a few minutes each day to be present and tap into what you are grateful for.

Look ahead by creating a cup list (my version of the bigger bucket list) ... write down something you'd really like to do that would make you happy that is achievable each day or week, then take steps to accomplish one.

When you feel an unwelcome emotion, do a shame check. Scan to see if it's the healthy updated shame operating system or the outdated unhealthy version. Be curious and gentle with yourself.

Take actions to support you by reaching out to someone you trust, or go find a mirror and talk to yourself. (It works.) Remember, you are designed to speak about shame because then your brain starts to numb the pain!

Practice taking deep breaths, closing your eyes and do the following exercise from *Authentic Alignment: Heart of Shame*. Picture yourself when you were a child. Take a moment to experience it. Add yourself in now as an adult who wraps their arms around little you. Then speak to shame so that your little self hears. Something like—"Unhealthy shame I don't need you now and I will be responsible from now on, and protect myself." Tell the voice of unhealthy shame whatever you need it to hear. This helps little you to un-attach from the unhealthy shame. Tell your critical voice that you are strong, wise, and you can never be alone because you love yourself. Speak your hurt and acknowledge your feelings as both the mature you and little you. Tell little you that he/she is loved and able to make her/his own choices safely. Check in with how you feel when you finally have said what you need to say and open your eyes.

***

To Contact Michelle:

Phone: (914) 471-5712

Website: Directimpactnow.org

Twitter: @Dune63

Facebook; https://facebook.com/MichelleGesky

Or ask her any questions at Michelle@directimpactnow.org

Stuart Elliott

My name is Stuart Elliott. I am a transformation catalyst who specializes in helping people look where they normally wouldn't so they can unearth their hidden resources, find the answers that they already carry, hidden away, and apply them to their challenges and transform their lives.

You see, when you take a fresh new look at any challenge you may face, you will be surprised at the unique solutions you come up with to conquer your challenges.

I have helped many people from all walks of life unearth their hidden stores of confidence and seen them grow from success to success... Now it is your turn!

Building Core Confidence

By Stuart Elliott

Welcome—in this chapter, you are going to walk step by step toward becoming a new, super confident you. A person who is no longer afraid to tackle new things or walk down the street or even go about your daily life.

There are five main areas to focus upon when you want to uncover your Core Confidence and become a super confident person who is always in charge.

These are:

1. Clarify or create a clear vision of what you really want to achieve—instead of saying you want to 'be more confident' you will uncover how, when, or in what way you want to be more confident.

2. Strategize your actions—create a plan that you can follow so that you build confidence daily.

3. Upgrade your skills—once you have the skills to do things, then you feel more confident about doing them. Further, once you understand that you can learn to do things, this will also boost your confidence.

4. Optimize your environment—if your confidence issue is connected to weight or dress, for instance, it will be difficult to change if you do not get rid of all the things around you that contribute to your issue. This could mean discarding the chocolate or chips or even changing your clothing

wardrobe… and you know how wearing fresh new clothes makes you feel good.

5. Master your psychology or thinking—helping you release your fears, doubts, limiting beliefs, and insecurities and help you to create confidence through new empowering beliefs.

Once you understand and master these five key areas, you will understand what you truly want and have a path or a system to follow so you can achieve your desires and grow to be the super-confident person everyone looks up to.

Now, you will only get out of this chapter what you put in, so if you only read it without completing the exercises and thinking deeply about your life, you will not achieve significant results.

STEP 1: Clarify and Create A Clear Vision of What You Want To Achieve

Before you can start to 'fix any problem,' you have to know what the issue is. Now, everybody faces challenges in their life. Some of these challenges are shrugged off like water off a duck's back, but others can stick around a little longer.

The thing is, though, some of the challenges we face can be hidden from plain sight. Maybe the mind doesn't want to deal with them 'right now,' so it files them away for later… but, as you know, later often doesn't come because something more pressing steps in. And the result is you have all these 'little challenges' waiting to be solved and, because they aren't dealt with, they can coalesce into one big challenge that can sap your confidence.

For this reason, we are going to spend a little time delving down into what challenge it is that you really want to fix. It is no good trying to simply 'be more confident.'

You need to get specific here—Confident when? In what way?

And, once you get down to the root challenge and fix that, you will often find the other challenges just fall away through the 'domino effect.' It really is quite satisfying and very liberating when that happens.

Now, it is important that you take the time to answer the following questions fully (write them down!). Some of the answers you find might surprise you!

- ❖ What is it about yourself that makes you think you lack confidence? - Think deeply about this question and write down anything that comes to mind. You see, there could be more than one thing that is causing you to feel this way. It could be a situation like giving a speech or when meeting new people or something about the way you dress that 'just doesn't feel right.'

- ❖ How specifically do you feel in that situation? - Be honest with yourself here; maybe you would like to run away and hide or, perhaps, you pretend you are invisible. If you feel uncomfortable think deeper—what specifically are you uncomfortable about?

- ❖ How would you like to feel in that situation? - Imagine yourself being 'super-confident' with all the poise in the world and notice how you would react differently to each situation you mentioned above. If you would feel like a King, write it down and then think about how a King would feel.

- ❖ What is preventing you from becoming this behavior for each situation? - If you can imagine yourself feeling that way, then you CAN feel that way. You may need to change something to get there, say you think a King has nice clothes... What is preventing you from getting nice clothes? Perhaps you want them, but don't have the finances right now, so you need to concentrate on getting a little more money to buy just one item, for now…

- ❖ Or maybe you are not sure what suits you. In that case, you need to find someone to advise you on the 'look' that really suits you, makes you feel confident, and makes people feel confident being with you.

- ❖ What you are looking for here are all the excuses you make that keep you trapped in the "I can't" thinking. Once you've identified the excuses, you can change things and become an "I CAN!"

- ❖ What, specifically, do you want to change about your confidence levels? - OK, so you say you lack confidence, but what is it you really want instead? How do you really want to feel instead of just 'confident'? Think about it and write it down—be as specific as possible.

- ❖ What would this change mean to you? - This is important, if you just shrug this question off with "Oh, I would feel confident and happier," then you are not going to get far. You need to be as detailed and specific as possible because you are looking for reasons to change. Without a reason, change is impossible; you simply won't have the motivation.

- ❖ How would your life be different with the change? - Think about this. How would your daily routine be different? What would you do differently from day to day? Would you get up earlier or eat differently, or enjoy yourself more?

- ❖ If you could be one person in the world, who would that person be? - Everybody has an idol or idols whom they try to emulate

The Change[10]

or wish they could be like. They could be living people or people already passed away... And don't stop with one person either; you could like one thing about person 'A', another about person 'B', and so on. Write down their names.

❖ What, specifically, is it that you admire about this person? - Now, think about the names on your list from above and start to jot down all the things you admire about them.

❖ How could you 'borrow' that admirable trait and embed it into your own personality? - The key here is NOT to try to become your idol, but to take the part of his/her personality that you admire and build it into your daily life.

❖ Now imagine your life with ALL these changes in your confidence in place. - Take some time to see yourself living your new life. Really experience this new, confident you.

Now it is time to make a plan and take some action!
You see, dreaming about your new life, and imagining you are super-confident is not enough. You have to start doing something right away to make those dreams come true. And, perhaps I can hear an excuse building up here... Maybe you think the change is too big, that you won't be able to do the things necessary... Well you are WRONG!

You only need to start with a small step, something that is easily manageable and things will snowball from there. You will feel more confident, people will start to notice and praise you, which will give you the confidence to do more, and soon your old patterns will fall away. They will be replaced with fresh new patterns of confidence—all from one little change!

Imagine you are out for a walk and you notice a big rock at the top of a hill and, just for fun, you want to see if you can push it down. It looks big and heavy, but you try anyway. You give it a little push and slowly it starts to move… You stand back in amazement as you see the little change you introduced create a massive reaction and the rock gathers speed as it thunders away down the hill.

This is the effect you are going to have on your confidence when you make one little change.

STEP 2: Strategize Your Actions

OK, now that you have a list of things that you want to change and how you want to feel in different situations, it is time to get organized and implement the changes. You may have listed many things and feel a little daunted at the prospect, but that's OK…

You see, once you organize things, you will see how many fit together with the result that fixing one issue will cure a whole host of issues.

The first step is to start grouping the things for commonality and you will likely find a lot of repetition here. Just group them all together: take a fresh sheet of paper and make lists of the things you want to change.

Once you have done that, spend some time thinking about what is most important for you to work on right now. When you take things one at a time, it is much easier to get great results and, as we saw earlier, great results will snowball into greater results, which means gaining confidence will give you more confidence!

OK, now that you have identified the challenge that is most important to work on right now, it is time to make a plan and list all the steps you need to do to achieve that goal. It could be that you lack something or maybe you need to start making changes to your lifestyle, i.e., diet. No matter what, just list it and plan to get or do it.

Now that you have your action list, take a look at it and answer the following question:

"What is the smallest step I can take right now that will start me off to achieve my change?"

Remember the big rock you pushed before? It only took a little effort to make a big change, didn't it? This is what we are looking for here—the smallest thing you can do right now to get started. The rest will take care of itself once you get started.

That's all you have to do… Just get started!

STEP 3: Upgrade Your Skills

Perhaps on your list you put "but I don't know how to do that…" no problem! This is part of your strategy. Once you have identified what it is you need to do or learn, you can start to do just that.

If there is some knowledge or a skill you need to get or develop, think about how you can do so.

Can you get the knowledge from the Internet? Or perhaps you know someone who can help. Maybe your work has a training program or a friendly colleague who will show you the ropes.

Start to do some research and identify how you can upgrade your skill set. As you do so, notice what resistance rises in you (it could be in the form of an objection) and note it down so you can conquer it.

You must remember that you have spent many years practicing your bad habits, so it will take some awareness and effort to conquer your fears and develop new habits.

Got your plan? Great!

Now, what is the smallest thing you can do right now to get started?

Identify it and get started…

STEP 4: Optimize Your Environment

Whether you realize it or not, your immediate environment has a major impact on your life and willingness to change and become more confident.

Take a person who lacks confidence because they are a little overweight, for example. If that person has loads of cookies, crisps, chocolate, and other unhealthy, fattening foods in the cupboard, then they would find it very difficult to lose any weight.

You see, the temptation to take a small piece of chocolate, because it is there, would be too much. They'd rationalize the decision with all sorts of excuses, but in reality it's part of their old habit, so it would be difficult to break free and change to a slimmer, healthier person.

So now that you have your goals and action plan, you need to take a good look at your environment and ask yourself:

"How, specifically, does this reinforce my old habits and prevent me from becoming confident?"

Be honest with your assessment and plan to make changes where possible. For instance, it may be relatively easy to clean out the cupboard and replace the junk food with healthy alternatives, whereas it could be more difficult to throw out the TV if you are a couch potato who plonks themselves in front of it all day…

However, with a little ingenuity and knowledge of your unhealthy routines/patterns, you will be able to create fresh new ones that will contribute to your increased confidence levels.

And it will be fun too, so why not give it a go right now? Don't try and change the whole world from the outset either. Again, start with something small and manageable that you can quite easily do and build from there.

Another good thing to introduce into your environment is a success diary.

This could be in the form of little 'post its' that you stick on your fridge or around the house where they are visible to you and make you smile every time you see them: or it could be a traditional diary or journal that you complete every day.

You could also write success notes that you mail to yourself whenever you have had success and get pleasure from receiving. The thing to do is get creative in the ways you do this. Friends and family can help here.

If you go for the traditional diary, do make sure you MAKE a regular time to complete it and review it every day. It's OK to jot something meaningful down when it happens, but without a regular habit of, say, reviewing it at 10 p.m. each night, it can easily be forgotten.

You might think to yourself that "I'm tired now, but will remember to do it tomorrow morning." The thing is, though, tomorrow brings its own issues, so you put it off again and again until many days have passed without an entry or a glance.

Success is a habit…

Just as lack of confidence is. So why practice your bad habits and reinforce them when you can create success habits that bring you confidence?

STEP 5: Master Your Psychology Or Thinking

Confidence is nothing but sheer belief in your abilities or credentials. It is the hallmark of any successful person who makes it big in life. Confidence drives you to achieve and realize your dreams and ambitions. It makes you feel motivated and inspired.

Confidence makes you positive about your chances of realizing any goal successfully. It is associated with an optimist, generally someone who looks at a half-filled glass of water as half full rather than half empty.

In the words of Vince Lombardi, "Confidence is contagious and so is lack of confidence." If you stay in the company of people who lack self-esteem or confidence, it can make you feel really low in confidence. Whereas when you are in the vicinity of confident people, you are likely to be confident yourself.

Well now is the time to change that habit! Now you are going to start building and reinforcing good, confident habits.

The more confident you become, the more you will smile and enjoy life…

After all, you can choose to be unhappy or choose to be happy—personally, I choose to be happy…

In fact, I have made it a habit. Why don't you do the same right now?

All you need to do is look at ALL the things you can do and feel pride in what you have achieved.

Next Steps

These are quite simple…

What you need to do is go through all the notes you have taken and decide in what situation your confidence becomes a challenge, choose how you would like to react instead, and then determine the smallest thing you can do right now to achieve that change.

Once you have done that, take your 'Success Diary' and write it down. As you do so, feel some pride in your achievement because you are one step closer to becoming supercharged with confidence.

After you have completed this step, look at the next smallest thing you can do right now and repeat the process.

As you continue with this, you will feel your confidence building and the satisfaction of getting nearer to the person you are going to become makes you happier. Anytime you want to boost those feelings, all you have to do is check your success diary to see how far you've come.

***

To Contact Stuart

Web: http://doubleccoaching.com

Email: stuart@doubleccoaching.com

Katie Macks

Audiences intently listen when Katie Macks speaks. She quickly connects with people, holding them full of possibilities. Katie inspires new perspectives, incorporating Heart and Glow to show individuals that they can make the changes they desire in their lives. Katie believes that when people become aware of the attitudes, assumptions, and beliefs that drive their choices, they open up to possibilities they did not know they had. Katie is committed to uplifting the lives of individuals by assisting them in realizing that they matter and they can achieve their goals and have the life they want.

With a degree in psychology, Katie worked as a leadership trainer for a San Francisco company. In her thirties, she put her business career on hold to follow a dream. Katie embarked on a three-year solo journey around the world, primarily traveling to developing countries, and was graced by private meetings with Mother Theresa and the Dalai Lama of Mongolia.

Katie is a Certified Relationship Coach and the founder and owner of Get Your Glow On, LLC. She facilitates glow-shops, group trainings, and works one-on-one. Her mission: *Get Your Glow On* engages and empowers growth-oriented individuals to live authentic and accountable lives, making conscious choices that are aligned with their truth and heart, thus creating a ripple effect of purposeful connection and meaning in the world.

A Glowing Road Trip

By Katie Macks

Early in our lives, we are all faced with events and circumstances that changed our perceptions, not only of ourselves, but also of others and of the world. As we begin to grow up, the inevitable happens. These events and circumstances that occurred unexpectedly rocked our sense of security and safety. None of us were equipped as young children to understand or navigate through these life-changing events and circumstances that took place. We didn't have the resources or ability to discern the reality of what had taken place. Instead, we did the best we could as we watched and observed what was unfolding in our lives. We began to interpret these events so that somehow we could make sense of what had happened in order to figure out a way to feel safe, to be understood, and to still have a sense of belonging. Unfortunately, we were not able to perceive, understand, or assess accurately about what had occurred. At this very moment, we began to lose our sense of self as we developed into what we perceived to be the new truth about who we thought we were and who we thought we were not.

When was the last time you truly felt free? Another way of asking this question is, when was the last time you felt free from your thoughts? Does your mind hold you hostage with thoughts of not being enough—not good enough, not smart enough, not capable enough, not rich enough, not thin enough, not beautiful enough? How about thoughts of doubt? Who am I to be doing this or that, or, how about being held hostage to those back and forth negotiations with yourself? When I lose those 20 pounds, I will buy new clothes, or take that trip that I've been dreaming of. Another negotiation may be, when I have more education, degrees, or certifications, I will be worthy of doing what I love. I hold back because I fear that people will judge me not worthy, legitimate, or qualified until I have those initials next to my name.

Most of us have unknowingly been on a road trip, based on our life experience and based on what we have learned and perceived. I would also venture to say that most of us haven't really questioned how we ended up on the road that we're on. As a matter of fact, most of us have followed a road that seemed to be expected of us by our families, our culture, and our society. Inevitably, though, there does come a time in our life when we question the path or road on which we're traveling.

Truth be told, we have all been on our own road trip our entire life, but the road trip we've been on often lacks in accountability. What I mean is that most of us have either handed over the keys to someone else because it is just too painful to drive through our own confusion and discomfort in life, or we've ended up in these unexpected places, not knowing how we got there and what to do once we've arrived. Few of us were given the tools to navigate the terrain of our lives. For example, when we took our driving test, we showed the instructor, who got into our car, that we could do the basics such as following the designated rules so that we could get the perceived prize of freedom to drive on our own. This instructor then decides if we are capable of driving off the lot on our own. The challenge, as in life, is that we only learned the basic mechanical maneuvers, like stopping behind a white line at a stoplight or stop sign or learning how to parallel park between two cars. As long as we were able to perform those specific moves that were predetermined for us, we were then given the prize of being able to drive by ourselves. Once we passed the test, we were now on our own without any manual for what is in store for us; however, we drive off with the notion of what is culturally expected of us.

The Change[10]

Somewhere down the road, most of us end up in a place where we ask ourselves: How did I get here? How can I get out of here?

Many years ago, I realized that I was on someone else's road trip and working very hard to navigate the map that was designated by others for me. I knew it was time to create my own map. I took a bold stand for my life and decided to exit the road that I was on so that I could choose a new direction for which I was inspired. This realization didn't come to me with ease. Oh no, I suffered for years, denying myself from my hopes and dreams. Instead, I unknowingly ended up on the road to "success," not necessarily my own definition of success, but the success defined by others. All of a sudden, I realized that I was on the road to building financial security, which we are taught to aspire to and to follow. I was in a career that was very competitive, but the rewards and stakes were high if you made it to the top. I was a real estate agent and I worked day and night to get to the Promised Land of what success looks like in our culture. I made more money than I ever had. I bought my first home. I worked seven days a week, proving to myself and others that maybe, just maybe, I could find some self-worth through my results. I also hoped that I would be noticed and recognized for all of my efforts. I lived in a state of exhaustion and I wore that exhaustion as a status symbol of success. I had finally hit the big leagues, or so I thought. The reality was that I became a sacrificial lamb to my duties and obligations. I was hoping that I would be acknowledged at some level for my sacrifice and for my relentless efforts to find solutions and garner more business, all in the name of being a top producer in my field. I was driven to get to that so-called Promised Land of "being somebody" by following those unspoken rules of what many people call success. I had it all and yet my deep dark secret was that I was in agony. I felt alone, resentful, victimized by my life's circumstances. My life was passing by me and it had me by the throat. I had given up everything, most importantly, my time, in order to live the dream. It was the dream that I was taught to value. In order to be someone, I needed to fulfill the unspoken expectations of my family and my culture. I will let you know that it was very difficult to get off this so-called road to success. My agony began to engulf my spirit and I became hopeless. My thoughts were keeping me prisoner to the very circumstances that I could only wish to change. I wanted someone to lift me out of my misery. I was blind to the fact that my agony and misery were self-inflicted. I wanted to be rescued and taken care of; I was lost on this road, and yet anyone looking in from the outside saw a competent, driven, and successful woman who was putting her stake in the ground in that ever revered Promised Land. I felt desperately alone and lonely because I was working so hard to uphold the image that I had been projecting to world. Behind closed doors, I was crumbling. That in itself was exhausting, let alone the hours of work that I was putting in every day. Needless to say, I felt like an imposter because what I projected to the world was not the world in which I was living.

Finally, after many years of traveling on the same painstaking road, I took a turn and reached out to some people from my past with whom I had lost touch. I began the process of getting real with myself and I began to soul search. I was scared to face my fears because I had beliefs that there may be no other roads and no other options. I questioned—Is this all there is? Is this what life is really about? If the answer is yes, I thought it might be too much to bear, but I was willing to take the risk and search for new possibilities and answers.

At the age of 51, I begin again to create the road trip of my life by taking action and exploring new roads!!

Now, I want you to know that everyone had an opinion about my desire to reinvent my life. Unfortunately, there were many people, including myself, who had deep concerns and who flat-out condemned the road trip that I was about to take. Quite frankly, people were uneasy because I was about to leave the same road that we were all shared together. I was defying that unspoken agreement to suffer and endure. I got questions like—What are you thinking? You have a successful career, you're 51, what else can you do? How are you going to pay your mortgage and your bills? No one wants someone your age; you're all dried up. You can't start over again, not at this stage in your life. Are you ready to lose everything, you know that could happen, don't you? These conversations were daunting to say the least and they had an effect on me, but my pain continued and became my driving force to take the leap into the unknown, which brings me to today.

> "Success is liking yourself, liking what you do, and liking how you do it."-Maya Angelo

I am now 55 and I am on an entirely new trajectory. Prior to real estate, I was a leadership trainer and I remembered how much I loved working with people in the realm of possibility—the very thing that I lost when I was on the road to success. I decided to get my certification in Relationship Coaching. I now have my own business, Get Your Glow On, LLC. I provide trainings for individuals who are ready to take on the most important relationship they will EVER have, the relationship with themselves. The acronym for GLOW is Growing, Loving, Opening, and Willing, the qualities that are necessary to live an authentic life. Being lost on someone else's road has turned out to be my greatest gift because I am now able to work with and to assist people who got lost on their road, but are now ready to get back into the driver's seat and onto *their own* road trip!!

The deeper questions for you are: What do you want, I mean really want? and Are you open and willing to BE and DO what it takes to take the road trip of your life to your hopes, dreams, and desires?

Are you ready to get GLOWing? If the answer is yes, you are in for the ride of your life!! The good news is that this road trip doesn't have a defined destination, nor does it have a defined road map to get you to where you want to Glow. What makes this road trip distinct from any other trips that you've taken is that you design the route, the detours, the respites, the off-road adventures, and the speed at which you want to travel. There are no speed limits, so you can move at the pace that suits you. A heads up—when you choose to go off-road into mountainous regions, it may be bumpy, uncomfortable, and you may feel uncertain as you navigate areas that you couldn't even imagine. The beauty and excitement of going off-road is that despite the discomfort, you will find yourself in surprisingly beautiful and majestic areas, but always know that you have the option to get back onto a paved road that provides a little more predictability as you travel. The beauty of this road trip is that you are the one navigating. You choose the route, you choose the adventure, you choose it ALL!!

"I CHOOSE to live by choice, not by chance

>to be motivated, not manipulated

>to be useful, not used

>to make changes, not excuses

>to excel, not compete

>I choose self-esteem, not self-pity

>I choose to listen to my inner voice

>Not the random opinion of others."

-Unknown

The Change[10]

I have found so many amazing places along the way that have changed my life beyond my imagination. I have also driven into some challenging places that I found very difficult to get out of. I would love to share my findings and experience with you so that when you decide to get Glowing, you will have the opportunity to travel to these inspirational sites and maybe bypass some of the more challenging areas.

As I began my road trip, I realized that I needed to be mindful of the best choices I could make as I began my journey. I highly suggest that you start your journey in the Township of Consciousness. I was able to map out my first few stops, which helped me focus on where I wanted to go and what I wanted to experience.

Early into my road trip, I found a couple of adjoining towns that I hadn't planned on visiting, but they drew me in and they seemed inviting at first glance; however, I quickly learned that it was best to move through the town of Validation and the town of Approval quickly. Upon arrival, these towns looked open and welcoming, but I quickly found out that there wasn't much going on there because the people seemed to have outsourced themselves and their businesses. When I was in the town of Approval, I found myself seeking advice and acceptance rather than trusting myself as I was making my plans for my next stop on my journey. This felt all too familiar and the key was recognizing my own outsourcing. I suggest either passing through these two towns or if you need to, you can use them as a pit stop. Once I realized this, I got back on the road and headed out to my next desired destination. I found myself drawn to Confidence State Park. I choose a route that sounded beautiful and challenging to get to the park. I chose to drive through a coastal community called Brave Town. I found the drive to be exhilarating!! Brave Town runs along the cliffs of the Pacific Ocean. The only way in and out is on a one-lane road, with two-way traffic, along very steep cliffs. I wasn't sure how I would make it to Confidence State Park from Brave Town, but I did and I was thrilled that I managed the journey. Confidence State Park was everything I had hoped for. I spent much time hiking and camping as I reached every Peak and visited every Valley. I learned to appreciate the contrast of the mountain peaks and the valley floors. The range was humbling and there was great value experiencing the peaks and valleys. After learning more about myself, I was ready to move on to the State of Intention, but there were more beautiful areas along the way. I chose to drive through a region known as Bintheredonthat, which is on the way to my next stop, the beautiful mountain range of Vulnerability. I can't say enough about this mountain range. Not only did I find my voice in this mountainous region of Vulnerability, but I also found the courage to be seen and heard. I learned there is so much that I don't know and that being uncomfortable and uncertain in life is part of learning and growing on this amazing journey. This led me to the River of Surrender that flowed through the mountain range of Vulnerability. I was drawn to the river because it taught me about BEing. I could either fight the current or I could be in the flow. I am reminded here that there is nothing to fix within me or others. The river of Surrender is where I can let go of many things that get in my way, such as my assumptions, attitudes, and beliefs that I've made up over the years. My greatest lesson here was to see how my desire to be "right" about my beliefs gave me a false sense of power. I learned on the banks of this river that if I was willing to be curious rather than being "right," the world of possibility opened up to me. I learned to relax and let go of holding on so tight to what I thought was true. After learning these magnificent lessons, I chose to continue my journey to the State of Intention. I arrived here and have decided to stay. I am thoroughly enjoying what is unfolding here. Once I crossed the state line into Intention, I realized that if I focus my thoughts on what I want rather than what I don't want, I feel so much better and I am so much more likely to manifest what I want. Being clear about what I want and focusing on what I want has shifted my self-doubt and my uncertainty to joy and experiencing a sense of expansion in my life. As I was driving across the state line into Intention, I saw a compelling billboard that is a great reminder—"Our thoughts and feelings have an electromagnetic reality so manifest wisely."

I made the decision to hang out here in the State of Intention and I'm living in the beautiful City of Purpose and loving it.

One of the greatest lessons on my journey while living in the State of Intention is to accept uncertainty and the unknown. It is in this place that the mystery of life unfolds and creates unexpected magic. Living in this State reminds me that perfection is a myth and a distraction to getting to where you want to go. I encourage you to take the leap, and find the road that makes your heart GLOW!!

***

Direct: 510-847-9757

Email: katie@katiemacks.com

Follow me on Social -- Twitter: GetYouGlowOnUs

Facebook: https://www.facebook.com/KatieMacksCoaching

www.katiemacks.com

Calvin Carey

Calvin Carey is a world-class entrepreneur with an extensive experience; he has been in the business world for more than 25 years, where he performed at various levels within different top-notch companies. He started his legal courier service in 1989 and two years later, the Michigan Minority Business Development Council and Detroit Business Commerce named him Outstanding Entrepreneur of the Year and he was featured in *The Michigan Chronicle*. Calvin opened his investigation firm in 2005, Personal Injury Investigators LLC. In 1998, he was ordained as a Minister and in 2000, he became Pastor of Discipleship Ministries for two years.

Calvin's passion toward light led him to keep searching for true meaning about his purpose and it all came clear when he stumbled upon the documentary titled *What the Bleep Do We Know?* This changed his belief and he realized that life is more than he had imagined. In 2013, as part of his personal development program, he enrolled in Quantum Success Coaching Academy to receive a Certification as a Law of Attraction Life Coach. In 2014, Time Life Coaching was birthed during the coaching certification program. The acronym for "TIME" (Teaching Inspiring Motivating Empowering) you to live your best life.

Where Are You?

Looking at the world around you

By Calvin Carey

A child is born into a confusing world in which he/she may conform, with so many ways he/she sees which he/she should be. This question has been with me since my days in college. I have pondered this question for many years as well as its answer. And I have come to understand 95% of our population has no identity as to whom we really are. One night, I woke up in the early hours with a feeling of absolute fright. I had woken up with such a feeling many times before, but this time it was more intense than it had ever been. The silence of the night, the vague outlines of the furniture in the dark room, the distant noise of a passing train—everything felt so alien, so hostile, and so utterly meaningless that it created in me a deep loathing of the world. The most loathsome thing of all, however, was my own existence. What was the point in continuing to live with this burden of misery? Why carry on with this continuous struggle? I could feel that a deep longing for annihilation, for nonexistence, was now becoming much stronger than the instinctive desire to continue to live.

"I cannot live with myself any longer." This was the thought that kept repeating itself in my mind. Then suddenly, I became aware of what a peculiar thought it was. "Am I one or two? If I cannot live with myself, there must be two of me: the `I' and the `self' that `I' cannot live with." "Maybe," I thought, "only one of them is real."

I was so stunned by this strange realization that my mind stopped. I was fully conscious, but there were no more thoughts. I heard the words "resist nothing," as if spoken inside my chest. I could feel myself being sucked into a void. It felt as if the void was inside myself rather than outside. Suddenly, there was no more fear, and I let myself fall into that void. I have no recollection of what happened after that.

After I woke up that day, I walked around the city in utter amazement at the miracle of life on earth, as if I had just been born into this world. I knew, of course, that something profoundly significant had happened to me, but I didn't understand it at all. It wasn't until several years later that I realized that where I was resulted from a bad choice made by me.

The environment and people surrounding us, most times, influence and define who we are and who we will become. The most powerful influence on our personality or being is our mind—the voice inside our head. More emphasis is put on race, religion, and economics to position themselves. I've studied and watched people and have interviewed thousands as an investigator and what I have learned is that we have been programmed and we are under control by society's model of conditioning broadcasting networks. We have been born into this diverse world with many origins of people and cultures, countries, governments, religions, education systems, economic systems—the list goes on. I believe that our programming distorts the endowments of our abilities, gifts, and talents and our amazing God likeness, which I will address later in the chapter.

State of Brokenness

I'm reminded of a story in the gospels—the man at the pool of Bethesda that Jesus approached. The story talks about this marketplace where outside were five porches and a pool. People came and camped out waiting for the waters to be stirred supernaturally by a divine being. Jesus noticed this particular man out of several who lay out with a variety of conditions and knew he was in this predicament of default programming for 38 years. The

The Change

story states that angels would stir the waters during a particular season and whoever would enter into the water first would be healed of any condition of impotence. As Jesus walked by, he saw this man who was laid out on the hard uncomfortable ground, covered in dirt and seeming disoriented and lost. There were many people who were passing him by as if he was a fixture to the landscape that they often strolled through. His pitifulness and weak condition was that of a man who lay in a State of Brokenness. What occurred in his life that caused him to be paralyzed for 38 years? What caused his disability? Where did he come from? And how did he arrive there? Jesus asked the man if he wanted to be healed. The man replied, "I have no one." Jesus swept aside all superstition and bypassed altogether the need for magic water with one command: "Get up! Pick up your mat and walk" (John 5:8). The man was instantly cured, and "he picked up his mat and walked." The man did not need quicker reflexes or beneficent angels or enchanted water. The man needed Jesus.

Looking at this story, this man in question was faced with a big predicament. But still he didn't let his problem weigh him down. He sought for solutions to his problem. You could hear and feel the extent of his frustration when he said, "I have no one." Jesus was able to notice him due to his refusal to back down. He was in a State of total Brokenness, but yet he didn't give up. Where we are coming from should not influence what we get out of life. Your case may not be the same as the man at the pool of Bethesda. I use the man at the pool of Bethesda to talk about a person being in any condition for many years and being stuck and not having any support or anyone he could go to. The point I want to focus on is him saying, "I have no one."

Personally, I think that if where we are right now is unpleasant and we find ourselves helpless, it should be more reason for us to want to leave. The principle is the earnestness for change. Our lives should not be made to depend on the immediate help we could get. It only gives rise to unnecessary dependency. Most times, our fear of the unknown clouds and belittles our faith. The following are some of the reasons why people stay in their conditions and practice failure habits for years without realizing that they need to change and grow:

- Programming from birth
- Fear
- Belief systems

These three things affect the eight components of our image—Mental/intelligence, body/physical, spiritual, emotional, family relationships, Financial/income, career/ business, social. I believe that these are the dynamics that shape us in our everyday lives and it determines where we go in life.

In this world, broken things are despised and thrown out. Anything we no longer need, we throw away. Damaged goods are rejected, and that includes people. In marriage, when relationships break down, the tendency is to walk away and find someone new rather than work at reconciliation. The world is full of people with broken hearts, broken spirits, and broken relationships. To us, broken things are despised as worthless, but God can take what has been broken and remake it into something better, something that He can use for His glory. It all depends on whether or not we want that Change.

The open door to Change

A beggar had been sitting by the side of a road for over thirty years. One day, a stranger walked by. "Spare some change?" mumbled the beggar, mechanically holding out his old baseball cap. "I have nothing to give you," said the stranger. Then he asked:

The Change[10]

"What's that you are sitting on?" "Nothing," replied the beggar. "Just an old box. I have been sitting on it for as long as I can remember." "Ever looked inside?" asked the stranger. "No," said the beggar, "what's the point? There's nothing in there." "Have a look inside," insisted the stranger. The beggar managed to pry open the lid. With astonishment, disbelief, and elation, he saw that the box was filled with gold.

I am that stranger who has nothing to give you and who is telling you to look inside. Not inside any box, as in the parable, but somewhere even closer: inside yourself.

"But I am not a beggar," I can hear you say.

Those who have not found their true wealth, which is the radiant joy of Being and the deep, unshakable peace that comes with it, are beggars, even if they have great material wealth. They are looking outside for scraps of pleasure or fulfillment, for validation, security, or love, while they have a treasure within that not only includes all those things, but also is infinitely greater than anything the world can offer.

One thing you have to understand is that no matter the gravity of the problem you are facing, nothing is permanent. If there is the Will, there's always a way. If we are honest, most of us have problems like this, with things that disrupt how we perceive things, with people influencing how we do things, with life when it doesn't go the way we want it to go. All you need to do is to develop that hunger for a change. It's almost crazy to be doing the same thing over and over and expect to have a different result. That very moment you think all hope is lost, when you feel you have no one, when you are stuck in that awful predicament and it feels like there's no way out, that's when it really matters. There! That's the perfect time to look into the box!

The path back to the Yellow Brick Road

Time Life Coaching is the author's coaching program that is geared to bring instructional development for the purpose of finding meaning and change in their life to walk through the Open Door. I talk about the yellow bricks, which are the building blocks that you build down to get to Emerald City. Emerald City is that OPEN DOOR in the basement of your heart and soul, where there is a corridor with doors. Behind each door is an endowment of God's gifts to you for the world. These amazing endowments are waiting for you to discover. When you open the door, you realize that you are the Wizard and you are commanded to bring forth your wonderful creations to the world. Each individual requires the components that will allow him or her to get to activate their God likeness, which in turn allows you to open your door. Building blocks have been defined as decision blocks which require intended focus and have to be governed with actionable intelligence. Every day, we have the opportunity to make a decision to place that block to build the success stories to reach our goals and to live our dreams, but we must use our intention and pay attention to our focus on a day-to-day basis. It's important to realize that, just like when we learn any skill, we probably won't be good at this at first. Who is good when they are first learning to write, or read, or drive? No one that I know. Skills come with practice. Repetition is the mother of all skill. So when we first learn to go with the flow, we will mess up. We will stumble and fall. That's OK—it's part of the process. Just keep practicing, and you'll get the hang of it. Along the same lines, take things in small steps. Don't be scared to fail; everyone fails at something. We keep in mind that every decision, every step, and every move we make counts a lot, not just now, but in our nearest future. So we avoid complacency or any form of negative distractions. We must be focused and allow our decisions to be directed with legal brainpower as we place the blocks that build our success stories. And when we place each block with that intention, we will see the progress and development of our growth. So the purpose of these blocks is to build every day and focus on what we want and not what we don't want.

It's YOU It's TIME

***

To contact Calvin:

(248) 755-1141

ccarey@timelifecoaching.com

lifecoachcalvin@gmail.com

timelifecoaching.com

29193 Northwestern Highway Ste 550

Southfield, MI 48034

Afterword

Life is always a series of transitions... people, places, and things that shape who we are as individuals. Often, you never know that the next catalyst for change is around the corner.

Jim Britt and Jim Lutes have spent decades influencing individuals to blossom into the best version of themselves.

Allow all you have read in this book to create introspection and redirection if required. It's your journey to craft.

The Change is a series. A global movement. Watch for future releases and add them to your collection. If you know of anyone who would like to be considered as a co-author for a future book, have them email our offices at support@jimbritt.com.

The individual and combined works of Jim Britt and Jim Lutes have filled seminar rooms to maximum capacity and created a worldwide demand.

The blessings go both ways, as Jim and Jim are always willing students of life. Out of demand for life-changing programs and events, Jim and Jim conduct seminars worldwide.

To Schedule Jim Britt or Jim Lutes as your featured speaker at your next convention or special event, email: support@jimbritt.com

Master your moment as they become hours that become days.

Your legacy awaits.

Blessings,

Jim Britt and Jim Lutes

www.ingramcontent.com/pod-product-compliance
Lightning Source LLC
Chambersburg PA
CBHW052016070526
44584CB00016B/1783